NONE OF YOUR BUSINESS

None of Your Business

A WINNING APPROACH TO TURN
SERVICE PROVIDERS INTO ENTREPRENEURS

Shawn Dill & Lacey Book

LIONCREST
PUBLISHING

NONE OF YOUR BUSINESS

A Winning Approach to Turn Service Providers into Entrepreneurs

ISBN   978-1-5445-1371-3 *Paperback*
   978-1-5445-1370-6 *Ebook*

*For every super-talented service provider with a
conviction stronger than their desire to please...*

Contents

Introduction

It was 1996, New Year's Eve, approximately one year after I graduated from Logan University's College of Chiropractic and the first anniversary for my private practice in San José, Costa Rica. Outside of my apartment, the locals partied, preparing for the clock to strike midnight, when the real fun began. By all rights, I should have been outside celebrating with them.

I wasn't.

At twenty-four years old, as the owner of my own business, with no boss to tell me what to do, I should have been *leading* the festivities. After all, I'd made all the right decisions. The Clinton administration had made the move toward managed healthcare, and no one knew what the reimbursement landscape looked like for providers, but I had a pretty good idea. (I was twenty-four years-old, so, of course, I knew *everything*.)

I had decided that the best way to avoid the uncertainty of the managed-care environment was to practice outside of the United States. My initial plan took me to Nicaragua, but a friend there who also happened to be a high-ranking government official at the time advised me against starting a business there.

"If you like it here, head for Costa Rica," he said. So I did.

I didn't care that I didn't speak Spanish. I didn't care that there were maybe only five other chiropractors in the country and that even they weren't doing it full-time. It never occurred to me that because of that fact, most of the citizens didn't even know what chiropractic *was*.

What mattered was that I had been smart enough not to set up shop in the States during a potential reimbursement crisis for healthcare providers. I should have been living the life of a young, rich professional, enjoying the well-earned downtime, taking advantage of the spoils of owning my own practice.

I wasn't.

Instead, I went to bed early that night. Before that, I ate

the last of the beans and rice I'd purchased two weeks prior—beans and rice I'd bought by going grocery store to grocery store with garbage bags full of empty soda bottles in an attempt to collect my return deposit on them. I lay back in my bed, my stomach barely full, my head echoing with the same question.

How did I get here?

I had a vision of changing the world through healthcare. I was a talented clinician. Yet despite the managed-care changes implemented, my fellow graduates and peers were making it work stateside and making it work well. Granted, they had to play the insurance game in order to make it work, but I wasn't going to do that. I refused to "sell out." I was going to run my clinic with integrity and passion because I *knew* that that would be enough to be successful.

As I soon discovered, I couldn't have been more wrong.

At a time when everyone was tracking their appointments on PalmPilots, I kept a three-by-five scheduling book in my back pocket. That little notebook, sadly, was more than large enough to keep track of the *four* patients a day I was seeing. For those of you not in the healthcare profession, it's not uncommon for a provider to see four patients in an *hour*, let alone a day.

Lying there in my bed, hungry and broke, I knew I had to make a decision. I could throw in the towel, move back to the States, and learn the insurance game. I could educate myself on and enroll myself in HMOs, PPOs, and the assorted other alphabet-soup insurance plans. Doing so would make the dollars in my pocket practically guaranteed. My friends had been doing it with no small amount of success.

Personally, and professionally, I wasn't ready to pay that cost.

Giving up wasn't an option. I had too much drive to make my business succeed and too much passion to let go of my vision. I had come to Costa Rica specifically to *avoid* having third-party reimbursement providers dictate the type of care I would provide for my patients. Yet my passion for delivering the highest-quality care wasn't enough to achieve the level of success I'd imagined. There had to be better way.

There was.

I made the decision to use every resource available to me to get my name out into the community. I'd knock on every door, make every cold call I could possibly imagine. I did all of the "regular" things you're supposed to do: free spinal screenings, handing out business cards, and other "traditional" networking methods—all to no avail. Then, early in the new year, lightning struck.

I was invited to appear on the television show *Con Asombro*, hosted by Nono Antillon. The program was the Costa Rican equivalent of the *Today* show and represented an opportunity for massive exposure not only for me but for the field of chiropractic. I would finally have the opportunity to educate the public on the service I could provide for them, allowing me to help them in the way I had envisioned.

Problem was, I still spoke almost no Spanish. I prepared translations of answers to what I thought would be questions they'd ask: *What is chiropractic? What kind of conditions can chiropractic help?* I memorized the responses, confident that I'd perform well and take my practice to the next level.

She didn't ask any of the questions I'd anticipated. Not one.

True to form, I gave the answers I'd memorized, no matter what the question. I figured this was my only shot, so I was going to take it. Judging from the odd looks Nono gave me throughout the awkward interview, as I continued to provide answers for questions she didn't ask, I assumed that this was my first and last Costa Rican television appearance and that I had sunk my business. But I was wrong.

After the show, business picked up a bit. Then, about four months later, *Con Asombro* called and invited me back for another appearance. My Spanish had continued to improve, and the show went well—so well that they invited me back again and again, until I was appearing on the show once monthly. By the end of my second year, the practice was seeing two hundred patients per day, five days per week.

Eight years later, right before I left Costa Rica to return to the United States, I spoke with Nono at a going-away party. She recalled my first time on the show and told me that she didn't know what in the world I was talking about but that when she looked in my eyes, she saw something there—a story to tell. She told the producers, despite their initial protests, to bring me back, and to keep bringing me back until I got it right. She saw my passion for my profession and my desire to share that message with others.

She was right about that passion, that desire. But it took that first year of near failure for me to realize, both for myself and now you, that passion and desire aren't nearly enough to realize the success you envision.

WHY ISN'T THIS HAPPENING FOR ME?

Whether you're an allied healthcare provider, a massage therapist, or a hair salon owner, if you're reading this book, chances are better than average that you've asked yourself this question more times than you care to count. You're a service provider with a skillset that exceeds not only that of your peers but even some of your mentors and educators.

Beyond that, you've got a vision. You've got passion. You believe wholeheartedly that you can change the world for the better with the talents you have to offer. You've also seen yourself living the lifestyle of your dreams as a result of taking the risk of going it on your own, being your own boss, and answering to no one.

I believed all of that in my first year. Let's be honest, as service providers, we all believe, at one time or another, that if we just hang our shingle, people will come. The reality is that you need systems in order to be successful. You need systems and processes. You need marketing. In essence, you need to do all of the things you hate about business in order to be a successful independent service provider.

Take the most gifted clinician, better than the established best in the field and working for themselves. Because they avoid marketing and sales, because they lack the business acumen, they have no clients. They collect no revenue. No one knows them because the world doesn't know what they have to offer.

Sound familiar?

What you must realize is that, more often than not, wherever you trained to learn your craft taught you about your craft and your craft only. If you're a chef, you went to culinary art school to learn how to be the best chef you can be. They don't teach you how to run a restaurant. Massage therapy programs teach you about anatomy and varied techniques for relaxation. They don't teach you how to own and operate a day spa. If you're a hairstylist or an aesthetician, you went to beauty school to master the plethora of cuts and styles your customers demand. The school taught you nothing about how to maximize your client volume.

Your licensed, credentialed, and degreed providers are not exempt, either. As an attorney, you've mastered case law, precedents, and trial procedures. You didn't take one class that taught you the ins and outs of running a successful private practice. If you're a licensed physical therapist reading this book, chances are your program taught you the best in exercise science and manual therapy but gave you no insight into how to market to physicians and make your practice the choice of your community.

Having skill at your craft and a passion to provide it does not make a successful business. You need a bridge that brings those elements together.

LET'S BUILD A BRIDGE

Throughout this book, we are going to give you the tools to develop processes to run a successful business and the discipline to utilize them, based on lessons from our own successes (and, more importantly, our failures). From goal-setting the correct way to implementing strict time-management efficiencies, you will walk into your business the day after you finish this book ready to enact the strategies you learn here.

We're going to teach you how to convert your drive and passion for what you do into a sustainable, successful business by convincing you to embrace universal business concepts. We may even get you to love them.

You'll learn how to break down the stigmas around marketing and sales.

You'll understand the crucial difference between being your own boss and being a true entrepreneur.

We'll teach you how to adopt an abundance mindset that will allow you to serve more people to the absolute best of your ability and how wealthy clients aren't always necessarily the means to greater financial success.

We'll share all of these strategies and more so that you can realize the success I did once I came to embrace these concepts.

YEAH, BUT...WHO ARE WE?

Simply put, we're *you*.

Though our success has come in the field of chiropractic, we are service providers, just like you. We are those professionals who, at an early age, had a massive vision about how we could improve the world, who wanted every man, woman, and child to have access to a service we knew could help them. Starting out, though, we didn't have the tools to make that happen, and we learned the hard way what it meant to go without.

We don't want the same for you. We don't want the people who need your service to remain unserved. The idea that gifted, skilled, passionate providers have customers, clients, and patients who could be—who *should* be—benefiting from their services is a thought that keeps us both up at night.

Understand from the outset that this book doesn't offer

you a quick fix. There is no magic bullet within. You're not going to read the book, put it down, and go to work to find there is a line of clients out the door. This is also not an emergency room for your business. If you are a breath away from closing your doors, do not rely on the strategies here to keep that from happening.

We will not teach you about how to be better at what you do. You bring a level of skill that separates you from your peers, along with a passion that exceeds theirs. If you don't have that, we cannot give that to you. What you lack is the business acumen and the ability to bridge your skill and passion to it.

That we can give you.

One thing you must learn is how to utilize *discernment*—to choose the voice to which you'll listen. I'm a huge fan of mixed martial arts and the Ultimate Fighting Championship. I've been to a number of live events, and the crowd noise reaches an incredible level. Yet the fighters in the cage learn how to filter out the noise, to discern their coach's voice, to receive instruction from their most trusted adviser amid all the screaming and shouting.

Throughout this book, we ask you to see us as your trusted advisers. Listen for our voices through the din of countless other business books and internet advice about business that doesn't apply to your situation. The coach is free from the distraction of punches and kicks, giving him the ability to see opportunities for his fighter to take. While you're in the ring, we'll be shouting out strategies for you to take when the opening presents itself. That opening may not always be there. It will be up to you to make the decision of when to throw the knockout blow.

That's because this is a strategic book, not a tactical one. You will be able to take the strategies presented here and extrapolate tactics specific to your unique business. You will need to develop your own systems and processes, and our strategies will show you the way.

OKAY, YOU'RE READY. WHAT'S NEXT?

Even though you're reading this book, you might not think you have a problem in your business. The fact that you *are* reading this, however, says that you might. If so, the first step to solving that problem is to look inside yourself.

Many people go into business for themselves to be their own boss. In reality, all they've done is changed to whom they're responsible for their nine-to-five grind, which often means they're more lenient on themselves, ending up less successful than when they had a boss watching over them.

When I attempted to be my own boss, I failed in the same way. I had to discover what it meant to be an entrepreneur. To be more than just the boss. To understand that I had to wear multiple hats to reach as many people as possible while simultaneously running a successful business. To do things that pushed me out of comfortable places. Reaching out to television stations in Costa Rica wasn't an easy thing for me to do as a service provider, but I realized the value quite quickly. It was only then that I experienced a taste of what it meant to be an entrepreneur.

So, do you want to be a boss, or do you want to be an entrepreneur?

If it's the former, put the book down now. If it's the latter, then read on.

1

Are You an Entrepreneur?

"DID I SCREW UP?"

In the initial launch of my practice in Costa Rica, I had grand ideas of what it meant to be a business owner. I told myself, "I'm going to work three days a week, from 10:00 a.m. to 12:00 p.m. and then from 4:00 p.m. to 6:00 p.m., and that's how it's going to be."

Needless to say, that didn't quite work out. Once that realization set in, I had to figure how to make this work, and quickly.

At the time, I did not have children, but it was in my second year of practice that my daughter was born. She arrived in the midst of my business taking off, and I had to figure out how I was going to juggle that.

I've seen a number of female practitioners and service providers decide, and deservedly so, that after giving birth, they will not return to practice or their service. On the other hand, I've also seen quite a few who do come back, some part-time, others full-time. I often wondered what the differentiator was. Was the motivation financial? Were they driven by their passion to return? Did guilt, either internal or external, play a role?

It is typical, though not always fair, to assume that these decisions are easier for the father, but it is safe to say that many of them struggled with the decision to return to work as well. I did. I wanted nothing more than to be there with my children at every step, every stage of their development. I didn't want to miss their first steps or their first words.

As my business grew in that year, however, time slipped away. I worked 9:00 a.m. to 9:00 p.m. I lost time for even the simple things like getting a haircut, eating lunch, or going to the bank. In fact, when the clinic was at its busiest, I walked around Costa Rica with a messenger bag full of thousands of dollars of cash because I never had time to make a deposit.

In 2004, at the height of our success, we made the decision to move back to the States. We had thousands of dollars in liquid assets. We had four offices and employed six chiropractors and two medical doctors. I was involved in multiple other business ventures and had written the law that regulated chiropractic practice in Costa Rica. By all accounts, we were on top of the world. However, by that time, we'd had our second daughter, and they were ready to move into kindergarten and first grade. We wanted them to have a better education than was available for them in Costa Rica.

Moving back meant starting over professionally. I had to pass my national board certification exam. I needed to start a new clinic and manage all the details of getting it up and running. Every aspect of creating a business anew required a rebuild, and in doing so, I missed a countless number of my daughters' functions and life events. Talent shows, choir concerts, all without "Papi."

The thing is, it was intentional. I sacrificed my time at those events not because I had to but because I wanted to.

I knew it was a risk. I knew it was a gamble.

Yet because I chose to miss those events when they were younger, I was able to build a business such that, by the time they were in high school, I able to attend most, if not all, of the major events in their lives. My oldest daughter is a cheerleader, where there is an event or competition almost every weekend. I attend those now because I took the time earlier and built a business and a lifestyle that afford me the ability to do so.

Still, I wondered if I made the right choice for my daughters, so I asked them.

WHO ARE YOU DOING THIS FOR?

Before I tell you their answer, we want to ask a question of you. Better still, we want you to ask a question of yourself.

When you want to be there for those moments, are you doing it for your children, or are you doing it for yourself?

Let's be clear, we don't pose this question as a backhanded judgment. We ask this to make the distinction between being your own boss and being an entrepreneur crystal clear. If you want to be your own boss and create the flexibility that allows you to be there for those moments, that is a value-based decision that only you can make. You must be aware, however, that in doing so, you are playing the short game.

As an entrepreneur, you must play the long game. It is natural to feel guilt, especially in the moment, about missing out on key milestones in your child or children's lives, but if you embrace the long game, that you are doing this not only for your benefit but for your family, those for whom you're responsible financially, you understand why the sacrifice is all the more necessary.

Being an entrepreneur is a risky business, and it isn't for everyone. It has tremendous ups and considerable downs. Being your own boss or the employee of another boss is safer, by far. The financial growth curve that accompanies that choice is a slow, straight line up and to the right, provided you make the right decisions with your money.

As an entrepreneur, that growth curve is all over the page. The attraction here is that, at some point, you might find yourself on the highest of the high points, a level of financial success you might never achieve working under the "my own boss" mentality.

Those swings, though, come with no small measure of risk—time with your family being one of the most important to consider.

Consider this as well: Did you wake up today and think, "I should check out the internet today to see if there's an elementary school choir or band concert that's playing somewhere in town because I really want to hear it"? Of course not. You don't want to go to those things because the music is good, because, frankly speaking, it's terrible. You go because your child is participating, because somehow the music isn't so bad when they're performing.

We realized, in consulting with other practitioners in an effort to help them grow their businesses, that many of them had newborns, toddlers, and young kids, and they were so committed to attending those type of events. They told us what level they wanted to achieve with their business and how many hours they worked, but in the same breath, they told us that they had to be home by 5:00 p.m. every day because that's when the family sits down for dinner with the newborn at the table, because they put the baby down at 7:00 or 8:00 p.m., and it's important to them to be there for that.

Again, there is no judgment here. It is not a mistake to feel that way. However, if you're committed to being an entrepreneur, if you truly have the long game in your sights, then you have to ask yourself if you're doing these things for your child or for yourself.

Will your newborn remember the evenings you were home for dinner at the table? Will they recall the nights you lowered them into the crib for bedtime? Will they remember your face in the audience at their preschool holiday concert?

We don't ask this to be dismissive. Quite the opposite. In

fact, if you already know yourself to be an entrepreneur, we hope you find comfort in this, the idea that you can make a choice to miss these things, if you haven't been already, and that it's okay.

In all likelihood, your children won't remember those things. It's not something we like to face as parents, but it's true. Though it may be difficult to overcome the idea, the truth is that that forgotten time could have been spent building the business and creating a lifestyle for yourself and your family that allows you to be there when it counts—when they will remember.

This challenge is even greater if your spouse is not an entrepreneur, if their way of thinking is more in line with the nine-to-five. This difference in mindset creates great friction if they expect you to be at that concert, that talent show, or that T-ball game. I am fortunate in that Lacey is also an entrepreneur, but many others aren't quite so lucky. We'll talk about relationships later in the book and how developing the proper mindset as a team is crucial toward making any entrepreneurial venture work.

If you reconcile with yourself and, if need be, with your significant other that the long game is what matters, then you take one step closer to the realization that it is "okay" to be an entrepreneur.

A NOTE ON "HUSTLE AND GRIND"

This is a good opportunity for me to point out that I am a bit of a contrarian. I look at things with a different lens, and I am fully aware that, sometimes, my viewpoint is not always the most popular. However, that which is most popular is not always what is best or even true.

Having said that, let's talk a bit about the present entrepreneur culture.

It's popular now to be an entrepreneur. There are a number of personalities in the space. Some of them are celebrities in their own right, and as a result, they're glorifying the ends they've achieved, never the means it took to get them there. In that vein, it's equally popular to have a "side hustle," to be "on your grind."

Both as a consultant to service providers and as one myself, there are few concepts I disagree with more than the side hustle. If you're a service provider, you should have one hustle. I don't want to go to a cardiologist who does cardiology on the side.

I know that sounds flip, but it's true. Who wants to receive services from someone who does it on the side? For whom that service is not their calling?

Whatever it is you're passionate about doing, the thing

you were put on this earth to do, put it in the forefront. Attack it head-on. Make what you do what you stand for (something we'll address in the marketing chapter).

Next, the grind.

Your work, if it truly is your calling, should never feel like a grind. I've often heard the phrase, from colleagues and clients alike, that "they're in the trenches." A trench is just another word for a ditch. Why would you ever want to find yourself there if your work is something you truly love? If you are sacrificing time with your family and loved ones, do you really want to feel as though you're grinding it out at the bottom of the ditch? I'll never understand the motivation professionals find in this mentality.

To be an entrepreneur means you are creating a lifestyle, and there is glory in that, not in the grind. I don't "rise and grind." My workday typically begins at 12:00 p.m. I'm a member of our local country club, and I'm there almost every morning. As such, I've had comments made to me, on more than one occasion, that it must be nice to be so well-off to do that, that I don't ever work. What they don't realize is that when I return home by noon, I'm working until at least 11:00 p.m.

I don't feel for one minute that it's a grind. Never am I in a trench. I wake up every day and work hard. I bear arms for my mission and my vision, for the thing I champion for the world, because I believe in it, not just because it pays the bills. In turn, I am rewarded financially.

Chances are that, as you read this, you find that this resonates but not completely. You believe in what you do, but at the same time, you feel you are grinding. That you are struggling to make ends meet. That you're not being rewarded for your service and your passion.

I wrote this book for you.

IT'S NOT WHY, IT'S WHAT

Your first step in changing that is to realize that, in fact, you have been treating your business as though you were your own boss and not an entrepreneur. If you can accept that, then the next step is to tell yourself, and truly believe, that it is okay to be an entrepreneur as a service provider. Once you've done that, in order to make any strides, you must determine not your "why" but your "what."

When Simon Sinek's TED Talk was at the height of its popularity, I'd often attend conferences where speakers would begin presentations by talking about their "why." Invariably, they would show a picture of their family on the screen behind them. They expressed that they were there because they wanted to make the world a better place for them, that they were concerned for the future of their children. Of course, as a husband and parent, I understood that.

To a point.

If you're going to embrace entrepreneurship, you must ingrain in your mind that what people buy is not why you do what you do because everyone has a different reason for why they do it. Frankly, it's irrelevant. Customers, clients, and patients all will do business with you based on what you stand for.

I, Shawn Dill, stand for a world where health and success are known as fundamental truths rather than fundamental pursuits.

If you are reading this book, it is because you are in alignment with what I stand for, and I guarantee that if you distill down what you stand for, you'll find that every single person that does business with you does so because of that. I also guarantee that if you're reading this book, you cannot truly articulate that which you stand for, because you've only focused on your "why," which is, essentially, too superficial.

Once you determine your "what," it should permeate through every aspect of how you do business. It should be clear in the way you service your clients. It should be clear in your marketing and sales processes. It should be clear in the way you live your life. People will see it without you having to say it, and they will be drawn to your service. When that happens, you will realize that there are many people who share your vision and want to take part in that which you provide. This will allow you to grow your business, to grow your vision.

But you can't do that working three days a week, six hours a day.

A CHILD'S ANSWER

As a parent, you want to provide your child with a better life than the one you had. The problem is, there is no guide that tells you how to do that—no book that has a chapter on third-grade talent shows or high school break-ups. Believe me, I'd have bought it long ago. Because of that, up until the time my children were in middle school, I considered myself an epic failure as a parent. We had taken our children through some highs and lows in Costa Rica, then moved ourselves all back to the States, rebuilding amid some economic low points, and put it all back together again.

It was a relief to hear from both of my daughters that not only did they feel I hadn't made the wrong choice but that they were thankful. They weren't aware of the sacrifices of time at that young age, but they were quite aware of what those sacrifices meant for them today.

I'm a fan of a number of sports, and as such, I frequently make use of sports metaphors. Teams that try to win in the first quarter often lose the game. In golf, it is rare that the leader after the second round goes on to win. The halftime score of an NBA or NFL game rarely reflects the final outcome. When I look at my daughters, the eldest of whom is twenty-one, as they move into adulthood, despite times where we were down twenty points going into the second half, I feel like we won that game.

THIS IS YOUR JOURNEY

By now, you've made one of two decisions. Either you've put the book down because you are content to be your own boss, or you've slid your chips to the center of the table and gone all in on being an entrepreneur. Before we take this journey together, we want you to remember something of vital importance.

This is *your* journey.

There is an inherent danger of envy and comparison. All entrepreneurs are on their own unique path. One may have sold her business a month ago and is now flush with cash, living the high life. Had you met her six months prior, she might have been leveraging every dime she had, every minute of her day, to get to that point. If you had looked at my business a year in and not known any more about how I got to where I am, you wouldn't take one word of my advice.

Don't look left and right to see what the others are doing or, more importantly, how they are doing. We know plenty of people who drive extremely expensive cars yet rent their apartment or home. We know a number of individuals who wear suits off the rack but are multimillionaires. There is no time when one entrepreneur should be comparing themselves to another, even if they're in the exact same industry, because the timeline for success is different for everyone.

If you can do all of these things, then you're ready to begin the journey. The first step on the path toward entrepreneurship is to establish goals, but the right way. Let's talk about how to do just that.

2

Set the Destination

You're driving your car with the GPS running. You see yourself represented by a blue triangle, a dot, or some other icon that tells you exactly where you are on the map. But if you simply drive around, watching the arrow, you don't end up at a location. The GPS only tells you where you are, not where you're going.

Not until you set the destination.

Once you enter that information, the GPS provides you with turn-by-turn directions to reach that final location. Better still, if you choose to ignore the first set of directions it generates, it will determine a new path because now it knows what the end destination is supposed to be.

When it comes to their business, and specifically the

goals they set for their business, so many of our clients are simply driving around, looking at their icon on the screen, seeing only where they are and not where they are going. They know their revenue for the month was low, that they need more new clients, and that they need to decrease their spending.

They experience these challenges with their business because they don't have a clear vision of just what it is they're trying to create or why. In those cases, we'll pose the question "What would your life look like if you doubled your revenue?"

Without fail, the single most common answer we get to this question is: "A lot better than it looks right now."

Invariably, our response to them is this: "That answer is exactly why you'll never get there."

Hyperclarity is the key to effective goal-setting. It is not enough to say, "I want to make as much money as possible," or "I want to make enough to pay my bills." Goals that aren't specific are not goals at all.

THE SIX PS OF GOAL-SETTING

The foundation of our recommended process for goal-setting isn't revolutionary or even original to us. What is unique to our methodology is the way in which we guide our clients to utilize these principles in order to achieve their goals. We refer to them as the "Six Ps," and they are:

- Purpose
- Personal
- Professional
- People
- Prosperity
- Play

The first step in each of the categories is to write down your goals in that area.

For example, the goals you create under "Purpose" relate to what you consider your life's purpose, what you want to bring to the world, what you stand for.

"Personal" goals take the form of things such as a desire to lose weight, to wake up early each day for increased productivity, or to exercise more regularly.

"Professional" goals are of particular importance for the service provider who wants to excel in their business. As I continued to grow in my chiropractic career, I set a goal of serving on a professional board. I now serve on three: one for a research foundation, one for an international trade organization, and one for a chiropractic college.

Next, your "People" goals. Goals here are all about relationships. This refers not only to your significant other but perhaps to the community in which your business is located, your business colleague, and maybe even someone you don't know. Maybe you're reading this now and saying, "I wish I knew Shawn and Lacey better." Set it as a goal!

"Prosperity" goals are easy. What exact money goals do you have? How much do you want to make?

Finally, "Play." This is where you put all the fun stuff. The beach house, the Jet Skis, the planes, boats, cars, and vacations. All the things you want to do to enjoy yourself.

YOU CAN'T STOP THERE

For some of you, creating and documenting answers to the Six Ps is probably more than you've ever done when it comes to setting goals for yourself. You're not done yet, however. A few crucial elements remain.

- Write your goals in the affirmative.
- Time-stamp your goals.
- Determine obstacles to achieving your goals.
- Decide why you must achieve your goals.
- Maintain proximity to your goals.
- Keep moving the goalposts.

- Share your goals.
- Tie your goals to a reward.

First, you must write your goals in the affirmative. It's not "I want to make $500,000 in revenue." Instead, it must be "I *make* $500,000 in revenue" or "I *take* two vacations a year." The declarative nature of such affirmative statements has the effect of giving them authority in your mind.

Second, every goal must end in a "by when." They must be time-stamped. "I own two Jet Skis in the next three years." Be as realistic as possible here so that the goal is attainable.

The third step is a process that presents a challenge for many of our clients. You must write down every reason why you will *not* achieve your goal. For example, you establish the goal of losing fifty pounds, a goal you've established and achieved before, but you slipped and gained back sixty pounds. What identifying this does is makes you come to terms, in advance, with your potential obstacles. Doing so allows you to then plan for those obstacles in order to prevent failure before it occurs.

Just as important, list every reason why you *must* achieve the goal. This is vital because if you cannot come up with reasons why you must achieve it that outweigh the obstacles you foresee in your path, then you must remove that goal because it is simply not that important to you.

One of my "must" goals was membership in a country club. When I was seventeen years old, I shined shoes at a country club. I looked up to the success these men had achieved, and I knew then that I wanted that for myself. It was a measure of accomplishment I carried with me into adulthood, one that carried significant weight because it meant I had attained a certain status in my life.

Similarly, when I was financially able, I bought my father and myself a pair of matching Rolex watches. It was a sign not only to me but to my father that I had truly made it. I didn't want them simply because they were the cool thing to have or to make a statement to anyone else. They held a deeper meaning for both of us. That's what makes a goal a "must."

PROXIMITY TO YOUR GOALS

I am a big believer in the law of proximity. Once you've defined your goals and you're clear on them, then you want to surround yourself with the outcome as much as possible. If you want to make a half million dollars per year, spend time around people who make a half million dollars per year. If you want to drive an Aston Martin, go to the dealership and sit in one, test drive-one, be around Aston Martins in any way you can.

I told you I shined shoes at a country club, and as a result, I always wanted to belong to one. Ever since John Daly won the PGA championship, I wanted to move to Carmel, Indiana, and become a member at Crooked Stick Golf Club. While Lacey was born and raised in Silicon Valley, I eventually convinced her that it was the smart thing to do. We made the move and initially rented a townhome. We started there because we wanted to get our bearings and figure out exactly where we wanted to live.

It turned out Crooked Stick was going to be next to impossible to join that year because it was "invitation only." Though disappointed, I didn't want to wait, so I found another country club I liked and joined. While we rented our townhome, I kept an eye on the real estate market, and before I knew it, a house came up for sale that was directly across the street from the clubhouse of the country club I had just joined.

It seemed too good to be true, and in some ways it was. We had only been in our townhome for three months and could not get out of our lease. Before I went to the country club each day, I would drive to the home, just to look at it. When I left the club, I'd again drive by the house before driving home. I'd even gotten Lacey into the idea, having her make the trip with me whenever we attended the country club together. People must have thought we were casing the neighborhood. I continued to watch the home on Zillow, and they suddenly dropped the price by $50,000.

I convinced Lacey that we should go see the house with a realtor, and it was as perfect as it appeared on the website. We were determined to make an offer, and we did, one even lower than the asking price. After some negotiation, not only did they accept our offer, but we were able to get out of the lease on our townhome as well.

If you're old enough to remember a time before cell phones, you'll remember how, in an attempt to remember someone's phone number, you'd mimic dialing the numbers in the air. It was a form of neurological programming. I did the same thing by driving from the country club to that house, such that I did it almost on autopilot.

That's our law of proximity. We created a goal. We knew what we wanted, and we got as close to it as possible. That's what then allows that goal to become more real until it actually manifests itself.

So many people don't achieve their goal because they don't know what it looks like, and they don't know because they don't surround themselves with the outcome. When we ask a client what it will look like when they drive an Aston Martin and they answer that they don't know, that they just see them at the hotel valet and think they're nice cars, chances are slim that they will be able to see that through to fruition.

KEEP MOVING THE GOALPOSTS

When engaging in this exercise, do it in pencil. Goal-setting in this manner is plastic, fluid, and dynamic, not static. We've encountered a number of clients who love to establish their goals in December. They sit down on the thirty-first, write them down, and then check in a year later to see how they've done.

As you begin to approximate your goals, move the target out further. If I hit a single in baseball, I'm going to run it out. I don't run at first base and try to land on it. I'm allowed to run through, way past it, in fact, because if I wanted to stop, I'd have to slow down as I approached.

No one says, "I want to make $250,000 and then stop." If in October you made $240,000 and your goal was a quarter million, recalibrate and realize that you're averaging $24,000 per month and make $288,000 your new goal. The biggest mistake you can make is slowing down as you approach the goal, as you may very well end up falling short of your original intended amount.

SHARE YOUR GOALS

This is one of the most intimidating steps for our clients. Who wants to share their goals? What if they fail?

That's exactly the point.

Sit down with your significant other, a business partner, your operations manager, or anyone you might consider a trusted partner and say, "These are the goals I have to create." When you create goals in a vacuum, it's easy to make them fantastic and unrealistic. Sharing them with a reliable colleague ensures that you're held accountable to goals that are credible and time-stamped. Not only that, but now someone else will be there to remind you, "I thought you were going to make $500,000 by the end of this year?"

It is important to note at this point that all of the steps so far are not easy. In fact, it is quite difficult to set goals in this manner. We see our clients struggle with this depth of goal-setting often. At no point are you buying poster paper to put together a vision board full of magazine picture cutouts and setting it in a corner never to be addressed again. Accountability, realism, anticipating obstacles, and determining why you must succeed and why you might possibly fail are all quite challenging concepts and tasks.

There is one final step, however, that presents the greatest challenge of them all.

TIE YOUR GOAL TO A REWARD

Isn't the goal the reward? In some cases, yes. However, we also want to create rewards along the way—signals that serve as benchmarks to say, "I'm getting there." For example, if I say I want to make $500,000 a year, I set $100,000 in revenue as my first benchmark. At that point, I will buy myself that Rolex watch. When I reach $250,000, I buy a new car. When I get to $500,000, I take a trip around the world.

These benchmarks don't always have to be material. They can be experiences or doing things for other people. The point is not to tie the goal specifically to something financial but to link it to some type of reward, whatever that means for you.

Why is this so important? Recall that we talked about programming your neurology when it comes to your goals. Consider you've set a goal of collecting $45,000 in revenue in a month, and you fall short by $1,000. Then the next month, you collect $48,000. What happens to you in those two months is, essentially, nothing. Life looks no different at $44,000 than it does at $48,000. As a result, you unconsciously demotivate yourself because there is no real incentive for you to hit any of your goals.

To drive this home, we give our clients a simple exercise.

Set a goal, a very generic one as it relates to the larger ones for their business. We give them the example I use for myself: "If I manage my time properly for an entire week, I am going to buy myself a Ben & Jerry's chocolate chip cookie dough milkshake." If I stay on schedule all week, I get the reward.

Then I ask myself, "How does that feel?" What does it feel like to set the goal and hit it? What emotion does it invoke? It isn't enough to say it makes me feel good, because "good" is not an emotion. It makes me feel accomplished. It makes me feel confident.

Identifying an emotion tied to hitting a goal is a powerful tool because now I want to be able to cause that feeling on command. I want to elicit that emotion anytime I want because as I'm approaching my goal, I won't pump the brakes. I'll hit the accelerator. When I'm in proximity to my goal, I can now access the feeling of hitting that goal and drive forward until I achieve it.

As I've mentioned, I'm a big sports fan, and I see this phenomenon there quite often, For example, a golfer who has never won a major finally breaks through and does so. Next thing you know, he's won another. And another. And another. It isn't because he's necessarily gotten that much better at golf. It's because now he knows what it feels like to play that final round under pressure and win.

It becomes easier to repeat that performance because he can more easily access that feeling.

THE DESTINATION IS CLEAR

Let's go back to our GPS.

Remember that should you take an unexpected deviation from the course, the GPS will reroute you because it still knows the destination. This is the key to proper goal-setting. By establishing a clear objective, you will discover that while there may be detours, there is always more than one way to get there because you know exactly where you want to arrive.

Once you've plugged in your destination, the GPS also gives you an estimated time of arrival, or ETA. It will present you with a number of options and ask you if you want to take the fastest route. If you're like me, as you drive, you see how fast you can drive to trim time off the ETA.

In the next chapter, we'll discuss how effective time management can shave minutes from your ETA to achieve every one of your carefully planned goals.

3

Are We There Yet?

I have five email accounts linked to various businesses that I own. On any given day, I might receive upwards of three hundred emails. A vast majority of these may be nonsensical and of little value, but that doesn't stop them from landing in my inbox.

In speaking with my mentor, Jay Abraham, I mentioned this situation. He said, "Listen, why don't you delegate your emails to somebody who can read them, filter them, and respond in your voice so you don't spend so much time doing it yourself. It's eating away at your ability to get more important things done."

It made perfect sense. How much time do we spend just thinking about our emails? The notifications on our phones that let us know we have a new message? We open it with the intention of only reading one but then read five. We see an advertisement for a new tool or application for our business, and before we know it, we've fallen down the rabbit hole and lost more time than we can imagine.

Knowing all that, I was still quite resistant to Jay's idea. After all, who could read my emails? Who would I trust to access my accounts, let alone respond in my voice?

It was revealed to me that Gmail had a feature that allowed another user to view your email without giving away your credentials. They could log in with their own username and password, read your messages, and be set up such that they could respond as you, or as themselves, whichever the situation dictated.

When I realized this was not a novel concept, I researched the process of setting it up. I ultimately assigned my inbox to my assistant, who now curates my email. We have systems where she disposes of all the junk mail and answers questions to which she already knows the answers, such as dates on my travel itinerary. Anything that requires my direct response is placed in a folder called "Handle This Shawn." More often than not, I have five to six things that I actually need to see. I review them at the end of the day, address them as needed, then mark them as concluded for my assistant. Rinse, wash, repeat. In doing so, I have easily saved an hour and a half of work every day.

That equates to two additional coaching clients on my roster. If I only work coaching clients three days a week and add two of them on each of those days, making it six additional clients per week, then multiplied by four weeks, I'd see twenty-four *additional* clients per month, adding $48,000 in revenue.

What could you do with an additional ninety minutes *every day*?

TIME IS THE GREAT EQUALIZER

Everyone is afforded the same amount of time in a day. As such, you must develop an acute understanding of what your time is worth. It isn't enough to say "a lot." It is vital for you to calculate the value of your time by looking at your production. Look at the number of hours you provide your service and divide that into your revenue to determine one unit of what providing that service is worth.

$$Revenue \div Hours\ of\ Service = Value\ of\ Unit\ of\ Service$$

You should be pleasantly surprised with the value at which you arrived. However, many of you will also consider that because you're working sixty hours a week and not all of that is going toward providing a service, you are diminishing your hourly rate.

You'd be right.

Now we have an idea of what you're doing with your time, how to become more efficient with it, and how to increase your "hourly rate." Efficiency breeds success, and in order to become efficient, you must become obsessive about how you spend your time.

WRITE IT DOWN

All of it. Write down everything you do in a day.

Separate it out between the $20/hour tasks and the $1,000/hour tasks, whatever you determine your time is worth.

Then find a way to delegate the $20/hour tasks. There are a number of services available, including virtual assistants who provide reliable assistance for these types of tasks. If you're in the position to do so, hire a direct assistant who can handle any of the tasks that are not directly linked to generating revenue.

This begs the question, however, how would "Costa Rica Shawn," getting by on beans and rice, afford an assistant for these tasks?

It's a fair question, and the obvious answer is he wouldn't.

If there are financial limitations to delegating these tasks, then the answer is to be as efficient as you possibly can. Ensure that you are allocating the bulk of your time to $1,000/hour tasks. This will produce more revenue that will allow you to hire the necessary staff.

Lean business practices lead to this efficiency. Our business does not have one hundred employees. We staff as lean as possible. We have virtual assistants and ops teams. Keep your expenses as low as possible while freeing up your time to engage in your big-revenue-producing activities.

Keep in mind that there are things that you won't be able to delegate. These are the time vampires—like looking at Facebook or watching a television show. I began an episode of *Breaking Bad*, and I couldn't stop. The era of Netflix has made it such that you can sit down and watch ten hours of television in one fell swoop. I've done it, and I'm sure you have as well.

It is crucial that you develop the discipline to eliminate these vampires. The way to drive the stake through their heart? Write them down. Don't shy away from admitting how much time they suck from your productivity. It is an eye-opening exercise with tremendous results.

One of my most valuable time-management tools is the Book of Yet, and it has two sections.

One is a list of everything I have not done yet, consisting mostly of ideas that people have given me that I think are terrific and would like to one day implement. It helps me to avoid "shiny object syndrome." Oftentimes, someone will present me with one of these concepts that gets me excited but has no place in my current schedule, and so it will go in my Book of Yet.

The second section consists of ideas or concepts that I do not yet understand. Jay Abraham told me a story about a company that had been bought out by another, and as is so often the case, the new owners brought their own leadership. In addition, they brought in a fleet of luxury vehicles in which all of the leadership was transported by their own drivers.

A number of the employees soured on this concept and became quite vocal about it. The CEO explained that they had conducted an analysis of the commute time of their executives and discovered many of them traveled anywhere from one to two hours from home to work and back again. By giving them a driver, they were able to convert that commute into productive time for the company, which more than offset the costs of the cars and drivers. In fact, they saw a positive gain in revenue.

While the concept made sense, I was unable to reconcile it in my mind. Therefore, it went into my Book of Yet—have a driver to be more productive. While it doesn't fully resonate, because I documented it, there may come a time when I return to the concept when it does. In terms of the goal-setting we discussed in the previous chapter, this isn't yet a "must" goal. It's important enough, however, to warrant its own holding space, as it may elevate to "must" status as my business continues to grow.

Every Sunday, I review my Book of Yet. It is important for you to choose a day every week to review yours as well. Not all of your items are going to be as ambitious or on as grand a scale as hiring a driver. Perhaps you documented that your website needs an upgrade. With your weekly review, you will determine which of these ideas can be pulled from the book and be converted into action items for the week.

Once I've moved something from the Book of Yet into my agenda, I use the Passion Planner.

THE PASSION PLANNER

We were fortunate to have jumped onto the Passion Planner train early in its inception. It is an amazing tool for organizing your time. Planners and agendas are a dime a dozen, but the Passion Planner stands apart from the field because it helps you incorporate your goals and projects into your plan. This is not to say you can't use any planner to do this. However, because you will create a list with your own Book of Yet, it makes sense to use a tool where you can incorporate that list.

Utilizing the planner allows you to work in sprints, bite-size chunks or intervals of work, much like high-intensity training. With all of the distractions of notifications, texts, and emails, it's easy to argue that we are only capable of about to sixty to ninety minutes of intense concentration.

The idea that you should sit down and work on a project free of distraction for hours—that you sit down and work for that long, maintaining a continuous train of thought—is ludicrous. Knowing that fact, build your schedule such that service time is committed to first because that is when you will collect the highest revenue.

Then build in your ninety-minute sprints. Never go back-to-back with sprints, however. To use the earlier example, I will work on new website content for ninety minutes and set a timer. At the end of that time, no matter how much or how little progress I've made, I'll stop. If I finish before the alarm, I also stop. I don't attempt to do another project from the list.

If I have thirty minutes remaining, guess what? That's right. It's a reward to do whatever I choose with that time.

In fact, I create a competition with myself. If I can win thirty minutes of extra time eight times consecutively in a week by being efficient with my time, I've earned myself a round of golf. Just by being more efficient and productive, I've earned the opportunity to utilize that time however I want.

In that way, I never feel guilty when I play a round with my friends. I go so far as to include that time in my Passion Planner. I program in my service time, my sprints, and then any personal time, be it date night, family time, or that round of golf. Not only am I picking up time for myself, but I'm picking up time on my competition by being ruthlessly efficient with the manner in which I budget my time.

Make no mistake, there is a discipline to this, and it takes time to develop. It is similar to how it takes time to see results with dieting or exercise. We've seen it with a number of our clients. They will commit themselves to creating their lists and plans, but they go on vacation, and the discipline wanes. As a result, they find themselves back in an inefficient use of their time, and they have to make strides to course correct.

Fortunately, it takes little time to realize how much time you save when you utilize these concepts. Despite the notion that it seems restrictive to schedule everything, it creates a significant amount of freedom in my business and personal life, and it will do the same for you.

You are not too busy to do the things you enjoy. You just aren't efficient with your time.

BE JEALOUS OF YOUR TIME

To become more efficient with your time, you must treat it as if you're in an obsessive, jealous relationship with it. You check up on it every day. You tell it to text you when it gets to where it's going so you know where it is at all times. You don't ever want it to get away from you. It seems flip to frame it in this manner, but if you approach the investment of your time in this way, you will see the results immediately.

To that point, as you initiate these methods, we want you to document the accumulation of minutes, half hours, hours, and even days. Not only can you allocate them toward things like vacation and time on the links, but you can put that time back into your business.

Recall the example of bringing on an additional twenty-four clients by freeing up ninety minutes, three days per week. This is terrific in theory, but what if I don't have those additional clients waiting to be brought on? What if I freed up all this time and have no one to serve?

That's where a solid marketing plan comes into play, one unique to service providers, which we'll discuss in the next chapter.

4

Marketing

IT'S NOT JUST ABOUT WHAT YOU DO

When I opened that first clinic in Costa Rica, I was extremely passionate about chiropractic care. Yet that passion, that drive to provide the best possible care, did not convert to instant success. It made no sense. Why aren't patients knocking down my door for care? I am excited about chiropractic and they should know this. They should fundamentally understand this and want to do business with me.

Since that initial failure, I noticed, quite quickly, that I wasn't alone in this way of thinking. I also noticed that there are two distinct types of successful service providers.

The first servicer provider is "hyperdynamic." He has a

bigger-than-life personality, but the service he provides is, in actuality, not all that good. In fact, it is often quite mediocre, yet his personality overshadows his shortcomings as a provider simply because his clientele is attracted to his energy. He is a pleasure to be around and, as such, makes his clients feel as though he delivers excellence.

The second provider is "hyperdedicated." She is focused almost entirely on the craft of the service she provides, so much so that in the delivery of her service, she comes across as dry—the polar opposite of the hyperdynamic provider. However, because of her extreme competency, she is also highly successful. While her clients know they may not engage in entertaining conversation each time they see her, her appointment book remains full.

I discovered that in order for these two very different types to be successful, they have to have something in common. They have to be able to overcome any kind of personality deficiency or compensate for a lack of technical skill.

They have to identify what it is they stand for.

SIT DOWN TO TAKE A STAND

I am fascinated by Rosa Parks. It is fair to say I am somewhat obsessed with her story.

My fascination centers around the moment she made her decision to sit in the front of the bus instead of the back. Had she planned it prior to that day? Did she wear a particular outfit because she knew it had the potential for an incident that would make the news? Did she tell her family and friends, with anticipation, that her arrest was likely?

Or did she go to the bus stop like she had done every other day? Did she decide that today was the day when she'd say, "Not today"?

Did she decide in that moment that by choosing her seat, instead of having it chosen for her, she'd choose that for which she stood?

While we know more today about the history of the event, my fascination with the more commonly known story lies with the particular lesson I have drawn from it, which is this:

> History always remembers individuals who have a conviction stronger than their desire to please.

Rosa Parks wasn't the president, wasn't a leader. She was a seamstress who said, "Not today." She refused to please. As a provider, it is crucial to recognize that people are drawn to individuals who take a stand for something with which they can resonate. You don't have to be a leader or hold some other type of elevated status to do so. When you stand for something, you draw people to you.

WHAT IS YOUR STAND?

If we reflect on our own consumer habits, we see that we like to do business with companies or individuals who stand for things that resonate or are in alignment with our own habits and ways of thinking. For example, I like companies that are environmentally friendly. I like companies that treat their employees well, that are hip, that are consumer-centric. When you identify these things, you see that you aren't solely drawn to the service or product, but also to the essence of that for which they stand.

Marketing creates the awareness of who you are and what you have to offer the world.

FINDING YOUR IDEAL CLIENT

Once you know what you stand for, you are going to naturally attract people into your world. However, you may very well not like some of those coming through your door, and vice versa, even with your established commonalities. As a service provider, you only want to work with individuals who allow you to do your best work. Therefore, it is necessary to define your ideal client.

In the service industries, it is indisputable that there are some people with whom you enjoy working more than others. There are clients who, when you see them on your books, get you excited about providing them with your service. There are others, though, who ruin your day when you know that you'll be seeing them in the next few hours.

While the client might not necessarily know it, because you do a great job of convincing them that they're your favorite, at the end of the day in the quiet solitude of your bedroom at night, you admit that you don't do your best work with the people with whom you don't enjoy it.

So why not only work with those clients so you can provide your best service all the time?

When I was in Costa Rica, I had a good friend and chiropractor colleague across town. When I made the decision to leave for the States, he purchased my office. For approximately two months, we arranged a transition where I treated the patients while he was on-site meeting them. He maintained his other practice with the help of his wife, who was also a chiropractor. My practice was huge at that point, seeing more than two hundred patients per day. That volume of patient care dictated a certain pace, so patients who were slow-moving or who were needy, overly analytical, and asked a number of questions didn't fit the profile of my ideal client. We didn't have the time to have a thirty-minute discussion with a patient, because it would cause us to fall behind by ten to twelve patients, thereby affecting other patients' care.

One day during the transition, a patient told me he had some questions at the conclusion of his visit. I agreed, and his questions led to only more questions, and before long, that line of people began to form. I promised to set aside time to call him and answer his questions so that I could attend to my waiting patients. He agreed and left.

I turned to my colleague and said, "Now that you're taking over, where are we going to send all of the patients like that one?"

He responded with, "You dick. You've been sending me those types of patients all these years?"

"Absolutely," I told him. "Because patients like that are a good fit for you. I refuse to work with anyone who isn't for me. It doesn't mean I don't think they should receive chiropractic care. They just shouldn't receive it from me."

I can understand how this, in fact, seems like a dick move. It's not. A patient for whom I could not provide my absolute best service had been sent to someone who *could* do that for them. Not only that, but I was able to provide a referral to a trusted colleague, a patient who represented *his* ideal client.

This happens so frequently that it's likely it's happened to you at some point in your life, either in the retail or the service world.

Imagine you went to Nordstrom looking for a suit for an upcoming wedding. If they start showing you suits out of your price range and you ask them to show you something more in the $300 range, in all probability, they will send you elsewhere. It's not because they don't think you deserve a suit. It's because they aren't the best retailer for the product you desire. Conversely, because their suits are outside of your budget, you do not represent their ideal customer.

To put this in a service perspective, consider the client who doesn't respect your time. They've missed fourteen appointments, but they always reschedule when they do, just to miss that rescheduled visit as well. This might work fine if you operated a walk-in style business with open hours, and in fact, that would be the best fit for that client as well. In this case, it makes sense for you to refer them to another provider who, because that person represents their ideal client, can offer them their best service.

Joe Dispenza, author of *Evolve Your Brain*, discusses the observation that when children are at play, they lose track of all time and space. This phenomenon occurs for providers as well. It's likely you don't have to think too hard to recall those moments. You're working with a client, and when you look up, you're amazed at how much time has passed. Before you know it, it's lunch, when you feel like you arrived at work only an hour ago. Perhaps you forgot to eat lunch because you were so engaged in your work.

This is the environment you want to create for yourself every day. You can only do that by working consistently, if not exclusively, with your ideal clients—the customers with whom, when you're working with them, you are essentially entering a state of play.

Once you've identified the clients with whom you experience this, take note of their details.

- Were they male or female?
- Were they old or young?
- Were they well-paying clients?
- Did they have certain likes and dislikes similar to yours?
- Were they exceedingly respectful of your time?

Similarly, for those clients who create a feeling of intense dread when you see their name in your appointment book, you must define their common characteristics.

We realize that, in reality, the perfect client doesn't truly exist. However, we want to find clients who fall into certain ranges of tolerance. Clients who don't pay regularly and on time? I refuse to work with them. The serial appointment canceller? No thank you.

TARGET YOUR IDEAL CLIENT

By identifying your ideal client, you've now also identified your target market.

If I know my ideal client has two children in elementary school and is involved in school functions, my target market would be organizations like the PTA. If another shops at Nordstrom, drives a Porsche, and loves golf, I'd target the country clubs. Find where they are and target them where they live.

Too often, service providers try to capture their customers with too wide a net. Our healthcare-provider clients are notorious for this. When they tell us they've identified their ideal client, our next step is to ask them what they're going to do to get in front of them. Invariably, their answer is some form of free screening offered at a Walmart, Costco, or some other equivalent location where their ideal candidate isn't found. Yet they do it because that's what they've always done. It's what they know.

What they've always done is what brought them to us.

Once we've established that you must find your clients where they live, it's time to get your house in order. Charge a fee commiserate with the value of your service that the ideal client will pay. Fill the waiting room with magazines they read. Play the music they like. Tune the television to stations they watch. Create an environment based on what they appreciate and value.

One method we use to compile this information are focus groups. Gather a number of your ideal clients and have a third party interview them. This can be incredibly revealing, particularly when they are informed that their answers will be blinded, making them comfortable enough to give honest answers about you and your service to questions such as these:

- How do you feel about our price?
- How often do you utilize our website?
- Do you interact with our Facebook page?
- Is the environment of the office welcoming?

Not only do you obtain information about the office, but you receive important data about the allocation of your spending on strategies like website development and social media use.

Our gold-star method is a whiteboard we place in the waiting room. We write questions on it such as "What book are you currently reading?" or "What is your favorite restaurant?" and we allow clients to write their answers on the board. It's a fun and interactive activity while being a quick and easy method of data collection to improve our targeted marketing.

Finding out what books your clients read is a surprising source of information. We take the top ten books that our ideal clients read and search for them on Amazon. Then we read the reviews, with a focus on both the five stars and the one stars. I do this because people are emotionally charged when leaving either type of feedback. What I find by doing this is the language they utilize when they're in this state of elevated emotion.

For example, they might say, "This book revolutionized the way I looked at my business, and it gave me practical tips that help me grow and build a lifestyle of my dreams." In marketing my service, I will use that same language: "Come to our office, where we revolutionize the way you view healthcare." I use the negative reviews in the same manner. If one says, "This book was an utter waste of time, full of useless anecdotes," my marketing language will be "Come to our office where we promise not to waste your time with fluff and unnecessary conversation."

You can do this with restaurant reviews on Yelp, Google, and the like. The point is not to have your clients speak your language. You want to speak theirs.

YOUR COMPETITION DEFINES YOU

Most service providers wake up every day to provide their service to every person on the planet. In doing so, they feel a need to be all things to all people. Some clients want the stern physician; others want Patch Adams. The truth is that in order to provide their best service, they must be themselves. However, far too many entrepreneurs suffer from comparison syndrome.

Entrepreneurs, for the most part, are always looking over their shoulder at their competition to see exactly what it is they are doing. You must reframe that way of thinking. Your competition defines you.

Lacey and I noticed in our industry that that there were a number of emerging cliques that operated under an air of negativity. In those groups, the leader was right, and everyone else was wrong. That was the manner in which they built their businesses. They'd tell their consulting clients, "You don't know what you're talking about. If you did, you'd be successful. Now that we've established that, listen to me."

That didn't resonate with us. We created the Black Diamond Club to be the counterculture to that prevailing thought. We marketed ourselves as such. To that end, what our competition in the consulting space was doing defined us.

One of my favorite examples comes from a barbershop in Carmel, Indiana. They have a sign in their window that says, "We fix $10 haircuts."

That is the definition of letting your competition define you.

LEVERAGING YOUR STAND

Roy Williams is the author of the book *Pendulum*. In it, he discusses how, throughout recorded human history, societies have experienced twenty-year pendular swings. On one end of the pendulum, we tend toward an idealistic, "me-centric" society. At this stage, people strive to be more individualized and look to stand out from the crowd.

Then there is a twenty-year shift to a more neutral society, the bottom of the pendulum swing, and then another twenty-year shift to a community or "we-oriented" society, where people strive to fit in more than they do to stand out.

The good news is that, if you're reading this book within a reasonable amount of time since it was published, we are currently operating in a "we" society. The year 2023 will mark the peak of the "we" culture. With that knowledge, along with what we've discussed thus far, you can form your marketing strategies around the idea that people like to be around other people who are similar to them.

In a "we" culture, people want to be involved in a community and move the needle together. People change their Facebook profile photos during significant events in solidarity with people who reside at a large geographical distance—people they don't know but with whom they share a common stand. In making the move from marketing to selling, we must first build that community to leverage what you stand for.

We'll review some examples of that concept in chapter 5.

5

Building Community

There are few communities like CrossFit.

Of course, their fundamental essence is their trademark method of working out. Take a deeper look, however, and you'll see the undercurrent of a strong community. They wear a certain kind of athletic shoe. They began wearing colorful socks. Then they developed the CrossFit Games. Everyone chooses to participate because it makes them feel like they're part of something, and they strongly identify with what that something stands for.

The precursor to selling to your target market is to create the community. The community will develop an affinity for you as the leader, the glue that holds the group together. As such, they will be predisposed to utilizing your services.

One of our affiliates, Dr. Grant Dennis, with the Specific Chiropractic Centers in Little Rock, Arkansas, has done great work with this concept. His ideal client is a male hunter, a traditional classic sportsman. Admittedly, this seems like a broad market, difficult to target, but by leveraging this idea of community, he's become one of our most successful franchisees.

He created a group called the Society of Classic Gentlemen. He invites men of his community to come together for events like scotch tasting and educational sessions about cigars, fashion suits, different ways to tie a tie—all things that center around being a "distinguished gentleman." It started small, but grew quickly, because someone for whom all of this holds great appeal will leave an event and tell others they know. They will bring them to the next event.

When you create a group for community, be sure to have it meet regularly. Keep it a scheduled event, which participants can both plan for and look forward to. Make each event different. Don't give members an excuse not to attend an event because it was the same theme the month prior. Keep it fresh. In doing so, you'll discover something quite incredible! The community will go on without you.

Because of the regularity of the gathering, one fell on a

day when our franchisee was unable to attend. The group asked if he'd mind if they met in his absence. That they wanted to do so was a telltale sign that he had developed such a strong community that not only was it able to function without him, but that they didn't want to miss an opportunity to get together because they had developed an affinity for him and what he had created.

That affinity converts to business. Though these meetings have nothing to do with chiropractic services, he has built a strong community of his ideal clients who regularly engage with his care, who wouldn't think of going somewhere else for it. In fact, it's likely because these gatherings have nothing to do with chiropractic, not in spite of this, that he's so successful.

It is important to acknowledge that a group like this might seem almost too exclusive, in that it consists of only men. However, that is our franchisee's ideal client, the people who allow him to do his best work when they utilize his service. Another of our franchisees, Dr. Alex Nunn, created a group called Books & Bubbly, targeted at her ideal client, an audience that is almost exclusively female.

Would a woman be welcome at the Society of Classic Gentlemen? Certainly, though it's likely she wouldn't be comfortable. The same holds true for a man in attendance at Books & Bubbly. Creating a community means creating an environment that is welcoming for your ideal client.

BUILD TO SUIT

Once you build your community, you want your business to reflect that same welcoming environment.

Let's say your clientele consists primarily of high-ranking professionals—C-suite executives of corporations in your region. Because of their position, the majority of these individuals are going to come to your office either from 7:00 a.m. to 9:00 a.m. or from 5:00 p.m. to 8:00 p.m., so that is when you should maintain your hours to best serve them. The décor of your office should be plush with clean lines and with a large amount of white throughout.

As with the examples above, if a mechanic wearing a jumpsuit covered in motor oil and grease came into your office, would he feel comfortable? In all probability, he'd feel quite out of place because you didn't create that environment for him.

Some of you might experience some discomfort with this concept. Understand that you didn't create an environment such as this to exclude him, to drive him away, or to keep him from darkening your door. You built your office to suit your ideal client, the person with whom you do your best work. There is an office that is built to suit to the mechanic and those from his community in which your ideal client would feel equally uncomfortable. It is to that office where you would refer the mechanic because it is probable that he'll receive the best service from someone for whom he is the ideal client.

It's not always easy, or even feasible, for some service providers to engage at in-person events. Social media provides you with a number of ways to engage with your communities, as well as find potential members of a group you'd like to create, that are also quite effective.

Remember that we're in the swing of the pendulum where people want to belong to something, to be a part of something greater than themselves. As such, communities abound on social media. Mommy groups on Facebook. Football team fan pages. Accountability groups for weight loss and exercise. Search for these groups that comprise your ideal clientele, and build a community for them based on their commonalities.

It is also important to remember that in looking to belong to something greater, your community will look to that for which you say you stand. You must not lose sight of this.

The strength of the community you build will depend

on this. We created the Black Diamond Club as a group of service professionals who want to matter. By coming together, they matter more. What they resonate with is my statement:

> I, Shawn Dill, stand for a world where health and success are known as <u>fundamental truths</u> rather than fundamental pursuits.

You should craft your own statement now.

 Create your own movement, draw a community to it, and find the people who are in alignment with your vision. Once they are in alignment, they are only a step away from doing business with you.

CONVERTING COMMUNITY TO CLIENTS

All things being equal—and all things *not* being equal—people prefer to do business with those they like and trust. By this, we mean that if everything were the same, if two businesses presented the same qualifications to provide their service, if they advertised the same price and the same availability, the client would choose the provider they like the most.

Likewise, if everything is unequal, if one business is less available and more expensive, clients will still choose that service if the provider stands for something in which they feel an alignment. That is the tipping point.

Take Lululemon. They produce women's yoga pants that are arguably of inferior quality to some of their competitors' and are quite expensive, much more so than most other similar products. However, they have no issue selling them because their community loves what they offer. They aren't gauging their decision to buy based on technical data about the quality. They aren't making the purchase because it's affordable. They do it because they have created a community that puts them in alignment. Their friends wear it, so they have to buy it too.

Apple is another example. The iPhone has been pushed to the upper limits of pricing, and it simply doesn't matter. Regardless of when you read this book, we can say with a high degree of confidence that when the next iPhone comes out, no matter which iteration, no matter what the price point, there will be a line around the block to buy one. Apple has built an incredible community. What does that community do? They buy the newest product offering. When the next one comes out, they buy that. The core Apple community always buys the next new product. People in the Apple community are there because they like what Apple stands for. They are committed. You rarely meet someone who isn't Apple head to toe. They're either all in or all out. There is no in between.

Much like Lululemon, though, there are indications that Apple has an inferior design, in some ways, to that of their competitors. Their clients aren't buying that. They like the company's commitment to a sleek design, the artistry, and the user interface. Apple built a community full of their ideal clients, people who identify with their stance and have the money to afford their product. The phones have gotten so expensive that you now pay for the phone over the life of your wireless contract, and people do it without hesitation.

The question then becomes: How do you do this for your own business?

 AN INVITATION TO OUR COMMUNITY

Before we address that in the next chapter, we want to bring you back to the Black Diamond Club. The community that Lacey and I founded is full of leaders from a myriad of different service professions that come together because they resonate with what we stand for. As it has developed, it has learned to stand alone, much like the Society of Classic Gentlemen, and, as such, has formed its own lexicon and method of communicating.

As a fellow service provider, we invite you to come see what we're all about at BlackDiamondClub.com. There is a low barrier to entry, and it is the perfect place to dip your toe in the water to get a feel for the very things we've discussed not only in this chapter but throughout the book. Our biggest complaint? Members sometimes get overwhelmed by the amount of content that is delivered not by just me and Lacey but by the group itself. We have so many members from so many industries offering tips and asking and answering questions that it becomes a petri dish, a place to grow ideas to better serve your business. We hope to see you there.

Now that we've given you some strategies and concepts around building community, let's look at how we get them to become revenue-generating clients.

6

Sales

WHERE DO YOU WANT TO EAT TONIGHT?

Admit it. As a service provider, you thought about skipping this chapter.

We understand. You likely entered the service professions because you abhor selling. The fact is, though, you're always selling. Chances are that concept is nothing new to you. It's been said many times before: from the thirty-thousand-foot view, everything is sales.

It is vital to understand that, at both a high level and at the deepest fundamental one, it's true. Everyone has an agenda. Everyone is always positioning themselves to sell something, even if it's just an idea. We'll give an example that many, if not all, of you have experienced at some point in your lives. It's a question that conjures dread in all who hear it.

"Where do you want to eat tonight?"

BE DECISIVE

Of all the successful individuals with whom I work, decisiveness is their most common shared trait. Almost more important, they have the ability to make decisions quickly. That's not to say they arrive at them flippantly, but they have the ability to process information, sometimes in large amounts, at a higher rate of speed than competitors in their industry or comparable individuals.

This is important because we live in a world where the majority of people are not decisive. I contend that is one of the reasons why individuals are not where they want to be in their life, their career, or their business. They get muddled down in analytics, wanting to have all the information possible before making any kind of leap. They're waiting for infinite amounts of time they don't have for perfect.

Done is better than perfect.

It's important, then, to surround yourself with people who

are quick decision makers. You are the average of the five people you surround yourself with most. If you're averse to the risk that accompanies quick decisions, then you must condition yourself to the behavior by immersing yourself with those for whom it is second nature.

We travel often as part of our consulting work, and on many occasions, we find ourselves in new circles of people. One of the worst questions that comes up in those group settings is where everyone wants to eat that night.

One person suggests pizza, and a handful of others agree. Another objects and suggests sushi, and some of the pizza crowd have their vote swayed. Someone complains that sushi is too expensive, but that Thai sounds good. No, Thai is too much for someone's stomach, and on and on and on. Eventually a decision is made, but after much time lost, and no one is truly happy with the compromise.

CHANGE YOUR FRAME AROUND SALES

If you wholeheartedly believe that the service you provide has the potential to impact lives and change the world, you must pay attention to this chapter because absent sales, no one will simply adopt your way of thinking. No one is going to commit to your agenda. It's possible that they might engage your service at an arm's length, but you won't get the buy-in of your community or your ideal client unless you learn strong sales strategies.

Remember that marketing creates awareness, but it's never enough to just let them know that you exist. You must shift gears and sell your service, close the deal, and get them to utilize your services. To do that, however, you must shift the frame in which you think about sales.

Too frequently, we find that service providers treat sales like a dirty word. It's sleazy. It conjures the image of the stereotypical used-car salesman, looking to wheel and deal. That's not the frame we create for sales. Sales is persuasion. With that in mind, it's probable you've been pitched or sold to at least twenty-five times in the course of any given day, on a variety of things. That's because individuals, whether in a forceful or a passive nature, are in a habit of imposing their worldviews.

We all view the world through a certain lens, and it's natural for us to want others to do the same. It's true in general, and it's quite true specifically when it comes to the service various providers produce. If you're not willing to embrace some fundamental sales strategies, then the public's worldview gets imposed on you.

For example, some prospects will say that their previous service provider—be it their hairstylist, their landscaper, or what have you—only charged them X amount for their work. All too often, we see providers accommodate that because they assume the client's worldview that their prices are too high.

Another common imposition of worldview relates to the use of insurance versus cash for services. Insurance is the accepted method of payment for healthcare providers and has been for some time. As a result, providers have accepted this worldview and rarely consider the option of only accepting cash payments for services. We've encountered a number of younger providers who have been told by their mentors that they simply cannot survive in business that way, and so they only accept insurance when their profits could be so much higher with a cash-based business.

The simultaneous good news and bad news here is that views are not easily, if ever, changed. The way we look at the world is a by-product of our environment growing up, belief systems that surrounded us during our formative years, and experience. Those things become deeply ingrained. You have to look no further than a debate on social media as an example. Have you ever witnessed a discussion about political affiliations, gun control, or abortion end where someone says, "You know what? You're right. I've changed my mind."

The internet would explode.

As a sales strategy, recognize worldviews, but don't challenge them. Offer people a way for them to engage with you without having to sacrifice what they hold to be true. This is an essential first step in effective sales.

A prime example of this is the chiropractic stance on vaccinations.

We know a number of chiropractors who feel that the cost of vaccinations is not sound—that it's a flawed principle to inject you with a measured dose of a disease in order for your body to create the antibodies necessary to fight it. They feel that if the body already has the ability to fight it, then why introduce the disease in the first place? They take issue with the preservatives they feel are of a questionable chemical constitution contained within. In the face of research that they feel links vaccines to autism, they advocate for freedom of choice, even when evidence is arguably present that those not vaccinated are in danger from these same diseases.

These chiropractors, in an attempt to get people to access their services, entertained the vaccine debate. What happened as a result is that, at best, members of the public wondered if in order to engage chiropractic care they needed to renounce use of vaccines. At worst, for those who fundamentally endorse vaccination, they admonished, even ridiculed, chiropractic care.

They challenged a worldview, and it got them no closer to a sale.

THE BLACK DIAMOND CLUB SALES LADDER

- Build rapport
- Get permission to sell
- Qualify
- Build value
- Create desire
- Overcome objections in advance
- Present the offer
- Close with integrity
- Round and round
- The morning after

BUILD RAPPORT

Those chiropractors slipped on the first rung of the ladder. By attacking a worldview held by their potential clients, they failed to build rapport. Their method of attack involved educating their prospects, a key mistake and a barrier to building a connection with a potential client.

Two essential concepts to building rapport are:

- Empowerment
- No one makes decisions to look stupid

A majority of individuals walk around in a disempowered state because in most of their daily interactions, people are attempting to do just that: remove their power. As a result, often subconsciously, they employ strategies to return the favor.

For example, ask someone you know, "How are you today?" and they'll often respond with, "Eh, just another day. You know how it is, right?" That person is using the language of disempowerment. They want you to commiserate, to join them in their state.

We experience the same thing in the consulting world. We'll ask an existing client why we haven't seen them until now, and they'll respond with, "It's just been so busy; things just keep coming up." They want us to acknowledge and join them with, "Yeah, we hear you. We understand." They want us to engage them in a disempowered state, which is a terrible place to be when initiating a sales process.

Make your client feel empowered to make smart decisions about engaging in your service. Knocking them down and putting yourself in the driver's seat to make them vulnerable to a sale will have the opposite effect.

This brings us to the second concept. Never make people feel stupid for the choices they make.

You might not agree with their choice of diet or who they voted for, but making people feel "less than" for that choice creates an obvious barricade to rapport. It applies to the delivery of your service, as well. If you own a high-end salon and a client seeks you out because they received a poor manicure at a low-end price, you don't tell them, "Well, that's what you get."

Most people navigate the world doing the best they can with what they have. We need to recognize this in the initial phases of the sales ladder.

Join Existing Conversations

Once you recognize the importance of empowerment and lifting up clients based on their decisions, the next step in building rapport is to join existing conversations.

Imagine you're at an event or a conference where you see a presenter with whom you want to speak about your acupuncture business. He's speaking with a number of other people. You make your way up to the periphery of the circle. The presenter is discussing the Steelers as his favorite NFL team. There is a break in the conversation, and everyone turns to you. The first thing you say is, "Holy smokes, I sure love acupuncture."

It's funny to imagine, but as a speaker at numerous

venues, I've experienced this very circumstance. Invariably, someone takes this ham-handed approach to talking to me about their business. It's not that I don't want to hear about it. Quite the opposite. However, it's necessary to build rapport with me by finding a way to relate to the existing conversation.

The same holds true when selling your service to your ideal client. If you are that acupuncture practitioner and your ideal client is in conversation within their community about yoga, find a way to relate yoga to acupuncture. Speak to your experience treating yoga participants who were just starting out who injured themselves. Find a way to relate to them on their terms, not yours.

Know that rapport-building, along with the other steps in the ladder, almost never occurs in one interaction. Some of the stages may play themselves out over the course of days, months, or even years. If you provide a service that sells for $5 million, your sales cycle may take a few years before someone is ready to pull the trigger. Be prepared for the long game in building rapport.

GET PERMISSION TO SELL

Having said that, as quickly as you can, you want to move to the next rung: getting permission to sell.

Once you've joined the conversation, you want to control the direction of it. It's important to do this in an elegant fashion. Move it toward your focus by maintaining an interest in theirs.

Take the Steelers example. A more refined approach would be to say, "I'm a Cowboys fan myself, but one thing I love about the Steelers is that guy, James Harrison. He takes some creative approaches to treating injuries, and he's a big proponent of acupuncture. As long as they're not playing the Cowboys, I'll root for the Steelers just because of that."

This will pique curiosity, leading to the question, "Why is that so important?" to which, of course, the answer is, "Because I'm an acupuncturist." This is the beginning of establishing control of the conversation.

Understand, though, that in initiating control, you must remember to ask more than you talk. Don't talk about yourself more than you gather information about your prospect. You must do this on two levels:

- Do they have a problem I can solve?
- Are they a qualified candidate to engage in my service?

There are a number of factors that make a candidate qualified. Financial qualifications are obvious but others less so. For example, if your service requires multiple visits per week, someone that lives a considerable distance from your service would not be a good candidate. The previous worldview discussion also comes into play. If you are in significant malalignment, that person may also not present as a qualified candidate.

Once you've uncovered their fundamental problem to solve, your next step would be to say to them, "We see a number of people in your situation, and the work we do gets phenomenal results. Would you mind if I told you a little bit about our service?" You pose to them a situation in which you are now going to shift gears away from their existing conversation and toward your ask, your pitch. In doing so, you transition them into a sales conversation such that they don't feel they're being sold from the outset. It removes some of the sleazy salesman stigma.

QUALIFY THE PROSPECT

As you explain your service, you must also inform your potential client of what the commitments are to engaging your service, be they time-based or financial.

In the product-provider world, the transaction is quite simple: they give you money, you give them a product. In the service world, you provide an intangible. As a result, many service providers believe they are in a time-for-money arrangement. When you go to get your hair cut, you aren't putting the stylist on the clock. If the haircut took five minutes less than expected, you don't expect to pay them less, particularly if you're pleased with the results.

Along those lines, we challenge you to think in terms of this: that the real transaction that occurs in your business is one of reputation. Through the results you deliver, you offer up your reputation in exchange for the client's commitment. It is for this reason that you must qualify your candidates. If they can't afford you the time you need to deliver your best service, and if they simply cannot financially afford your best service, then they are not a qualified client.

Because you have the heart of a service provider, you will be tempted to make exceptions to this rule. As such, you must think of this exchange of services for time and money in terms of your reputation.

Reputation can be lost in a day. By not protecting it, you put your business at risk because one individual who didn't get the result they desired due to their not honoring their commitment will never, ever mention that to their friends and family when complaining. What they will talk about, though, is that said lack of results, thereby destroying any chance you have to sell to a new prospect who heard this information from what they consider a trusted source.

BUILD VALUE

Oftentimes, service providers do the exact opposite of this step. Instead, they offer massive discounts, coupons, Groupons, and the like. They devalue their service, when they should promote value versus discount.

If you run a nail salon and I'm a first-time client who comes in during a particular month, perhaps you give me a free one-hour massage, offered as an additional service. I would see that as a value-add. Not only do I have the opportunity to try your manicure and pedicure services, but I also have the chance to try the massage. If you truly trust in your offerings, you are confident that I'm going to enjoy both services and that I'm going to become a lifetime client for both. The value of that proposition is much higher than if you offer me twenty dollars off my manicure and pedicure. If I accept that offer, I might not even know you offer massage.

Pricing

In many cases, service providers are so severely underpriced that the proposition becomes almost unbelievable. The truth is that these severe discounts only speak to a section of the population, though service professionals tend to think they speak to everyone. It is a smaller section of the population than they expect, particularly when it comes to services. The average consumer does not know how much things actually cost. Consider *The Price Is Right*. It is baffling how many people don't know the costs of average items like a can of soup, a tube of toothpaste, or larger items like a propane gas grill.

Likewise, the average person has no idea how much a physical therapy treatment or a Reiki session or an MRI should cost if they haven't had it done in the past. They come up with a price in their head based on the value they place on the service considering their particular situation when in need of that service.

If you had an exposed nerve in your tooth and I asked you how much a root canal costs, what would you say? In all probability, you'd guess the price to be quite high, perhaps thousands of dollars. What, then, if I told you I had a dentist who would do it for fifty dollars? That rate is so low as to not be believed. You'd question the quality and the expertise of the provider based on your need for the service and the value you've placed on it.

I don't look for the cheapest dentist or the cheapest hairstylist. I don't want my golf instructor to be the cheapest if he's also the worst one.

Do not undervalue or underprice your offerings. Your clients' trust in your service depends on it.

Fill the Void

When it comes to value, there is an emotional void your prospect is looking to fill as well. How many of your clients come to you in spite of the service you offer, not only because of it? I'd venture you can list a few. They engage you because they like *you*: they like that you take the time to listen to them, they like your staff, and they like that you always have banana-nut muffins in the waiting room.

We find this in a number of our consulting clients who come to us not necessarily just to fix their business but to be heard. They have business issues to be sure, but no one is listening to them, leaving them with an emotional void they don't know how to fill. Many of them are struggling with personal problems that show up as business issues. We offer help that lets them leverage systems and processes that clean up their business, and they invariably report back that not only has that happened but that their relationships improved, that they were on the brink of divorce, and they saved their marriage.

That's building value.

CREATE DESIRE

Recall our discussion of the pendulum. We are currently entrenched in the community mindset. In this era, we need to speak more to emotion than to logic. In observing your prospects, you realize that they oftentimes engage in things that fill the aforementioned emotional void.

Your job is to show them you can fill that emotional void with your service; however—and this will be difficult to hear for some providers—your actual service will be the *secondary* reason why your clients engage with and return to you. What's less difficult to comprehend is that they will engage and return because they like you. As we discussed previously, people prefer to do business with those they like and trust.

Create in them the desire to utilize your services because you fill that emotional void, and you take another step up the sales ladder.

OVERCOME OBJECTIONS IN ADVANCE

Many sales strategy courses teach you to overcome objections, but almost always, they save that for the close. Your strategy, however, is going to be to head those off as soon as possible. We recognize that it isn't possible to overcome every objection your prospect might have. However, if you've tried selling in some form or another, you'll recognize common objections that will help you handle them when they arise.

The strategy we've found to be most effective is to voice the objection for them. For example, let's consider a client for whom you've built rapport. You've gotten their permission to sell to them, you've qualified them, you've identified that they want what you have, and you've created desire. They finally confirm to you that they want what you offer. Now is your time to tell them why they might *not* want your service.

> "If you are like most people, at this point you're probably worried about what my service might cost, especially when I've told you that I have a track record of increasing my client's revenue anywhere from 100 to 300 percent. Not to mention, there's a large group of documented testimonials from clients who attribute their success to me. Given that, you think this is going to cost you a ton of money."

Similarly, you know your clients might express concern with the time commitment for your service. Put it on the table before they do. Doing so strengthens the rapport you built in the first step. It tells the client, "Man, they get me. I'm not crazy for thinking this is a reason to say no." At that moment, reinforce their thinking by saying, "If I were in your shoes, I would probably be thinking the same thing."

Be careful with your word choice here because language is important. Of particular importance is the difference between "I hear you" and "I understand."

If someone voices an objection to your fee before you've voiced it for them, responding with, "I understand," triggers in their subconscious that you, in fact, understand that your fee is high and you agree, therefore validating their objection. If instead you respond with, "I hear you," you acknowledge the objection, which makes them feel listened to but then allows you to pivot.

> "I hear what you're saying. In fact, a number of people think that initially, particularly when they run a business like yours that's smaller in comparison to my other clients. Your being smaller, however, gives you the room to grow that the larger businesses might not have, allowing you to potentially see that 100, 300, even 500 percent increase in revenue. When that happens, you'll see my fee is actually quite fair."

Tell them you recognize their objection without agreeing with it. Counter with your expertise and results.

Another method to eliminate potential objections is to ask if they've ever tried your service from another provider. If they haven't, great. You're working with a clean slate. If they have, you need to take a slightly different approach.

First, ask about whom they received the service from. Be complimentary toward the provider because your process hinges upon coming from a place of integrity. You don't have to knock someone down in order to position yourself. Then ask two key questions:

- What did you love most about the service?
- What is one thing you would change about your previous experience?

When they tell you what they loved, it gives you the opportunity to overcome potential objections by reassuring them you offer all of those amenities and more, as long as that is true.

- The second question allows them to voice their potential price objection. If you happen to charge less than their previous provider, then you've got an easier conversation on your hands. If not, you can couch the objection with your expertise and value for your fee as above.

PRESENT THE OFFER

On the seventh rung, we make the offer. "Do you want to do this?" In some cases, you present this as a recommendation based on your process. If you're a physician, you might say, "Based on my exam findings and testing, I recommend this procedure."

Nice and straightforward. Keep it simple.

The offer should not be forced or unnatural. It's all about timing. It needs to be offered when the prospect asks for it. It shouldn't be scripted, as if you're following a sequence. It should be logical, effortless, and conversational. People will ask questions in which they are essentially asking you to close them. They give you an invitation to close them.

"What does it look like for me to work with you?"

To which your internal response should be: "Did you just ask me to close you?"

This is not where you begin to tell them the ins and outs of your company or what your process looks like. They don't want to know about any of that at this point. They've given you the invitation to close, and you must accept it by presenting them with an offer proportionate to the amount of trust you have built.

It is important to note that a number of our clients sometimes get hung up on the process of the sales ladder and get overly concerned when a prospect doesn't follow the steps in sequential order. Realize that the prospect isn't running themselves through the rungs. It's okay to skip steps.

Sometimes people step onto the lot prepared to buy a car. Don't miss or ignore subtle cues because they occurred out of order. Your prospects haven't read this book. They have no idea where they're "supposed" to be.

They've opened the door for you. Walk through it.

CLOSE WITH INTEGRITY

Clients have choices when it comes to the sales process. We don't want to be in the business of utilizing neurolinguistics programming or some form of hypnosis to trick our customers into engaging a service they don't need or for which they aren't appropriate. We want them to realize that the best thing for them is you and the service you provide.

This is a core principle. There is no "do" in this stage of the sales ladder. If you honestly believe that you are the best person to provide for your potential client, then you can't help but to close with integrity. This rung becomes a non-step because it happens as a matter of course.

"The best thing for you is me."

ROUND AND ROUND

Let us give you an example of what can happen with a specific offer on the table.

> "After going through this process with you, I'm going to rec-ommend that we work together for six months of coaching where I will work with you one-on-one every step of the way. There are several ways we can do this. You can pay the full amount up front, or, if it's more convenient for you, we can break that amount up into six payments every other month. Which of these options is going to work best for you?"

Then say nothing. Allow the prospect to work it through.

The axiom in the sales world is that the next one who speaks is going to buy. Either they're going to buy my service or I'm going to buy their objection. It goes deeper than that. Remember that we opened the chapter dis-cussing decisiveness and how most people don't make decisions quickly. We must be respectful of an individ-ual's process and give them space to decide. Give them time to sit with it, even if it takes uncomfortable minutes in silence to do so.

If they tell you they need a day to think about it, chances

are they aren't being truthful. In general, people make decisions such as these based on emotion—emotions you wanted to elicit when you created desire. If they tell you this, you failed to overcome an objection in advance that would have addressed this emotional need.

Similarly, if they tell you they need to discuss the offer with their spouse, then you missed an opportunity to head this objection off at the pass. You didn't obtain enough information while building rapport to determine if a spouse would need to be involved in a decision of this magnitude.

Realize that, at this stage, there may be objections you can neither anticipate nor combat.

Some prospects will just say no. They went through your process. They enjoyed your presentation, but they decide for themselves, despite all your due diligence and qualifying, that this service isn't for them.

Others will delay, telling you they recognize they need it, but not right now. Again, there isn't much you can do to redirect this objection. In fact, this may have resulted due to an inability to qualify their ability to commit either the time or finances to your service.

Still others will end up obtaining your services from a

direct competitor. Your sales process may have been flawless, but someone else held the trust and credibility commodity in greater supply than you. You closed, but you did it for your competitor.

Finally, there are those who realize they have a problem you can solve, but they choose an alternative method to solve it. For example, a client can realize they need chiropractic services, but they opt for physical therapy instead.

The key to avoiding these scenarios lies in the rungs of the ladder leading up to this point. Ensure that you complete all those steps, and if in doing so, you find that you cannot create desire, you cannot build rapport, or any of the other necessary steps, you must move on to the next prospect.

THE MORNING AFTER

The adrenaline rush of the close is a very real phenomenon. It's so powerful that it makes you forget about the morning after, the crucial time when people who make a decision of any magnitude tend to second-guess what they've done. They'll ask themselves repeatedly if they did the right thing.

Do not allow your sales process to end with the close. The effectiveness of a simple email, thanking them for their choice and reassuring them of their decision, cannot be overestimated. Equally useful are small gifts that speak to them as an individual, to some detail you discovered about them while building rapport.

This can come the literal day after or a week or even a month later. However, we'd also argue that your "mornings after" should be continual.

There is always competition for your service. The minute you stop validating your client's decision to choose you, they will look elsewhere, and your competitors will be more than happy to ask your client for a shot. Create the feeling in your client that would never allow them to consider leaving by continually reassuring them that they are in the best hands when they are with you.

REMEMBER YOUR COMMUNITY

Everyone in the community you built is somewhere on this ladder. As an exercise, we want you to go through and determine which rung on the ladder they occupy. In doing so, you will identify what steps to take next with them because the process is linear and sequential.

In dealing with clients, the very definition of *overwhelm* for them is when they don't know what the next logical step in the process is. In my work as a consultant, it is my duty to help my client discover what that next logical step is so they can make their decisions from a well-informed place. Don't just always be closing. Always be clear.

SO WHERE DO YOU WANT TO EAT?

Lacey is a vegetarian, whereas I love a good steak. As you can imagine, where we go for dinner touches every rung of the sales ladder. Observe.

Build rapport. "Hey, do you want to have dinner tonight?

Get permission to sell. "Do you want me to choose?"

Qualify the prospect. "Were you thinking something quick, or do you want to go somewhere nice?"

Build value. "There's this amazing steak house that's been getting rave reviews."

Create desire. "They have an extensive menu. I've already checked it out online."

Overcome objections in advance. "I know it's a steak

house, but what's cool is they have a number of vegetarian dishes on there, and the Yelp reviews about them are stellar."

Present the offer. "Would you like for me to call and see if we can get a table?" Then I wait.

She says yes.

Close with integrity. "Great. I'll make the call."

Round and round. "What should I wear? Do I have the right clothes? Do we even have time to get there?"

The morning after. "How good was that dinner? Thank you so much for letting me choose."

WHAT ARE YOU AFRAID OF?

So many service providers are resistant to the sales process because they fear rejection. It's not that their fear isn't valid but that they need to reframe what exactly it is that they fear. We'll dissect that in the next chapter.

7

Rejection

DON'T TAKE IT SO PERSONALLY

Service professionals are deeply tied to their service. They believe it has the potential to impact people's lives and that they have a moral obligation to share their service with the world. When they see people in their communities who are suffering, they realize that if they do nothing to inform them of their services, they are making a decision not to share their offering with the world. They make a conscious choice to exclude those people from the possibility of experiencing what it is they have to provide for humanity. As such, when a prospective client tells them no, it is almost impossible to not take it personally, to not see it as a reflection of them as a human being.

What you must remember is that they are not saying no to you as a person. They're only saying no to the opportunity.

THE GAME OF NO

We encourage our clients to engage in an exercise, a contest of sorts, even if it's just with themselves. You must go out, sales ladder in your arsenal, and see how many nos you can get by the end of the day.

In doing so, you are presenting people with an opportunity of which they may not have been aware. So often, our clients tell us, "People just don't get it. They don't get what I'm offering." It's not that they don't get it. They've never had the opportunity to get it. As a result, in attempting to get these nos, you will invariably get someone who has been waiting for your opportunity to say yes.

Another reason a prospect might tell you no is because the opportunity isn't right for them *at the time* the offer is presented. Sometimes, an offer may not fit that client's worldview in that particular moment. Time passes and they mature as individuals. Perhaps they experience some setbacks that cause them to see that things aren't how they thought they were. When that happens, even if you don't happen to be standing in front of them at the time, that opportunity you presented still exists.

If you didn't make the offer a one-time deal.

Because service providers personalize rejection so deeply, they often write off a prospect when they decline the offer. They make up in their mind that "no" now means "no" forever. Some take it so personally that they, in some sense, withhold it from the client. If you don't want it now, then you can never have it.

WOULD YOU LIKE A REFILL?

Imagine you are a server in a restaurant. You are taking care of a table of four, and they all decided they'd have iced tea, and over the course of the meal, you continually refilled their drinks. As the meal comes to a close, you ask if you can bring them dessert. They say no. You then ask if you can bring them another round of iced teas. Again, they say no.

You leave to prepare their final check. When you return, they say, "You know what, we will take a look at that dessert menu and have a refill on our tea."

Does it make sense to tell them, "No, sorry, you said no already, and you missed your chance?"

Of course it doesn't. But that is what happens when service providers take rejection personally, when they mistake the "no" as a rejection of them, not the opportunity.

Another key factor to rejection is that the prospect might not understand the opportunity. They read into it much more deeply than you intended, and it's often because, as a service provider, you present the offer as an all-or-none approach. "Either you're going to come to me for the rest of your life and bring your spouse and entire family, or we're not working together at all."

You avoid this by being sure that, during your sales process, offers put in front of the prospect are always in accordance with the amount of trust you have gained in the relationship.

WHICH WAY WILL YOU SWIPE?

In the twenty-first century, the probability is high that most people are going to meet their future partner on some form of online platform. You create a profile with imagery that projects who you are and what you stand for. You don't want to post a picture of you leaning on a Ferrari with your shirt off if that's not your thing.

The written portion of the profile should then also truthfully reflect who you are and what you stand for. It would be inappropriate for it to say, "Do not reach out to me if you do not plan on being married in the next sixty days." Similarly, when you meet someone as a result of your profile, your proposition for your first date should not be a weekend getaway to some remote location.

Why? Because that sales offer—and that's what it is—does not match the amount of trust you have garnered in the relationship. The better move is for you to start with a meeting over coffee, where both of you have time to analyze each other, to see if your profiles are in alignment.

A strong relationship is built on trust. The way you earn that trust is by being who you said you were or doing what you said you were going to do. What happens in the coffee scenario is exactly what happens in the sales process for any service professional.

If I enter your massage studio for the first time, don't tell me about the promotion where I can buy sixty massages for only fifty dollars each when I haven't had the opportunity to experience your service yet. That offer does not match the amount of trust you've earned and will lead to rejection. Instead, offer me some type of value-add or a discount on the next massage. Offer a dinner date after coffee instead of suggesting the remote weekend trip.

We work exclusively with service providers because we're passionate about their passion. They believe their work has the potential to change someone's life or change the world if seen from a collective view. They're emotional. When they provide their service and please their client, the feeling is almost euphoric. Rejection then stimulates the exact opposite feeling in them because of that intense passion.

This lends to a degree of negative self-talk. If, out of one hundred prospects, ninety said no, you could take the position that you've earned 10 percent ROI on that initiative. So often, we see so many of our clients who focus on the ninety people they didn't bring in their doors. It goes the other way as well: if they sign ninety out of those one hundred, they find failure in the ten they missed.

Get in the habit of recounting all of the amazing changes in the lives you've touched every day. It is far too easy to forget the impact that you're having on your community.

LOSE THE GAME OF NO

The more qualified the prospect and the deeper the relationship you create, the less likely that individual is to say no. No matter how skilled you believe yourself to be with the cold sale, your likelihood of earning new clients who embrace your service with any degree of longevity using that strategy is 50 percent or less. You'll see clients with a high degree of buyer's remorse.

Male Mormons go on a mission for a year. They travel internationally to spread the word of their religion. On average, they convert one to two people per mission. They go out every day. They knock on countless doors.

They know in advance that most people are going to say no. It conditions them to handle rejection. It strengthens their conviction about what they do.

We want you to play that Game of No. Each day, we want you to aim for five rejections to every one new client. As with the missionaries, it will decrease your sensitivity to refusals and bolster your belief in the service you provide.

However, in aiming for those rejections, we want you to lose.

Let's revisit our sales ladder, specifically "overcoming objections in advance."

Analyze your objections, see if there is a common trend that leads to repeated rejections, and document them.

If, for example, one of them is price, a strategy to overcome the rejection might be to offer them some sampling of your service for free to qualify each other. Better still is to overcome that objection in advance once you've identified the common thread. If your service is healthcare, you might say:

"I want to tell you in advance that our analysis is one of the most advanced you'll experience. It is comprehensive, not only covering the basics of a physical exam, but we also perform specialized testing. Some people say the testing is pricey, but you'll find the results to be exactly what you need."

By documenting your rejection trends, you strengthen your ability to overcome objections in advance. You'll be losing the Game of No before you know it.

THINK YOU'RE READY? NOT QUITE

We've come a long way together thus far. At this point, you're feeling like you understand all of the concepts and strategies in this book. Perhaps you've set it down and gone off to implement some of them. You're marketing by creating awareness. You recognize your moral obligation to offer your services, and you've got your sales ladder on lock. You're embracing rejection. Still, there is something holding you back from realizing the success that you know you're capable of.

You have a terrible relationship with money. In the next chapter, we're going to fix that.

8

Money Mindset

I'm a big fan of a unique book called *The Little Money Bible*. I have it as an audiobook and listen to it often because I like to frame my mind around the thoughts and attitudes that I have relative to money.

I realized very early in my relationship with Lacey that we viewed money quite differently. She came from a nine-to-five family. Her father owned a landscaping company. While far from poor, they didn't have a surplus of money. They didn't take vacations. My parents also worked nine-to-five jobs, but they were upper middle class. We had the opportunity for nice things and trips.

Still, there were friends in my neighborhood who were much better off than we were. They wore Izod shirts and Jordache jeans, things that I wanted. If I was lucky, I got a pair of Jordache jeans for Christmas, but only the one pair. As when I shined shoes at the country club during my high school years, I gained an appreciation for the finer things. I'd watch these men come and go, obviously not working a standard eight-hour day, and said, "I want that. I want to know how I can get to that."

That was the birth of my entrepreneur mindset.

Lacey, though, was entrenched in another frame of mind. She began working at a movie theater when she was fourteen. Any money she earned went straight toward the family funds. Instead of designer jeans, she wanted a certain kind of lip gloss. In order to get that, she had to save for it.

This difference in our mindset continued when we got together. As we began our business relationship in tandem with our personal relationship, Lacey's viewpoint was to save whatever money came in. Put it away because it could *go* away at any time. Mine was, and continues to be, to spend it, though not on frivolous things. I wanted to invest it back in the business, to figure out how to capitalize on our revenue to make it more efficient and effective for us. In many ways, her view of money created a hindrance to attracting more of it.

RESISTANCE TO MONEY

There are numerous reasons why service providers might be resistant to money. One factor we see in so many of our clients is they feel they are not worthy of it. They often see other service providers in their field doing well financially and think they must be cheating. As such, they worry about what their peers and colleagues might think of them if they begin to do well.

Your colleagues don't pay the bills. If you are marketing and selling from a place of integrity, as we've discussed, and money is coming to you in abundance, there is absolutely nothing wrong with this. It is a reflection of how effective you are at bringing your service to the world. Embrace it.

You have to create space in your life to allow money to flow into it because it's all around you. Money is everywhere. It comes freely to you. Entrepreneurs don't live in a world where we trade time for money. That's for the nine-to-five crews—if you give me an hour, I'll give you twenty dollars. In our world, particularly the service world, it doesn't work that way. As a result, there's no limit.

Say you're an exceptional hairstylist, one of the best, and a movie star comes to you because his hair has been butchered and he has to be at the Oscars tonight. You can fix it, but you're going to charge $10,000 to fix it. Will he pay? Of course. What if you charge $25,000? $50,000? He's in. No limit. It's not about time or even results in exchange for money. It's about what he needs and what he values in that moment and if he can enter into a fair exchange with you.

THE UNIVERSE IS CALLING

Money is all around you, but you're not tuned in to it. I noticed that the more tuned in I am, the more aware I am that money is all around me. It just starts showing up. There is a concept in *The Little Money Bible* that money often shows up lying on the ground. Pennies, nickels, or even bills. I once had a discussion with a coaching client about the idea, and later that evening, he related to me that he looked between his bed and nightstand and found twenty-seven cents.

Bear with me on this one because it might seem a bit hokey, even a little weird, but I firmly believe the reason why to be this:

> The universe sends us tests to check our availability to receive.

I was walking with a good friend once in downtown Boston, and in the distance, I spotted a penny on the ground. This seems hard to believe, but when you're tuned in, you begin to spot coins on the street from a great distance away. I called my friend's attention to it, but he dismissed it as just a penny, and because I was with my friend, we walked past it. Not without some anxiety on my part, however.

In my mind, if the universe sends me one penny and I refuse it, I'm sending the message back that I'm good. I'm all set. The universe then won't only stop sending pennies but dollars, tens, twenties, or hundreds because I've closed myself off to the possibility of receiving more. I must be open to receiving money abundantly. I put that penny in my pocket to say to the universe that I'm open to more.

I say all this to say that you must be open to the idea of abundant money. When you're not open to receiving it, what you will tend to find in your marketing and sales is a resistance over price point. As you navigate your community, you will find a number of people who are afraid to invest in you and your service, who say you're too expensive because you project an energy that says you don't want it, you don't need it, you're good.

This applies to the idea of putting money away as well. If you don't spend it by investing in yourself, it's only natural that the prospects you encounter are going to have reservations about investing in you. You'll be left wondering why everyone is going to the competitor down the street who charges triple what you do when you provide the same service at the same level of quality or better.

AVOID THE POVERTY COMPLEX

Your clientele wants you to drive a nice car. We've spoken with so many clients who are afraid to do so because they think it sends the wrong message. That it tells their customers they must charge a significant amount for their service because of what they drive.

That is the poverty complex. That somehow you must appear to be doing poorly in order to seem accessible. The opposite is true. Put yourself in the consumer perspective. I don't want to go to a dentist who shows up to work in a decrepit vehicle. That signifies to me that he's not doing well financially, and the reason for that might be the quality of his service. I want to see him doing well because it means he'll do well for me.

We also encounter a number of providers who tell us that by pricing themselves high, they wouldn't be able to afford their own service. If you've just graduated medical school, completed your residency, and now you're a neurosurgeon, it's true that at this moment, you probably couldn't afford your service. However, the ability to afford your own service is no marker as to whether or not you're good enough to warrant the amount you charge for your service.

Additionally, as with the movie star in need of a stylist, chances are you could afford your service if you were in a position where you had to have it. If you have an exposed nerve root in your tooth, even if you don't have insurance, you're going to figure out how to get the money for that root canal. Even if you just graduated dental school and opened your practice today, you might not be able to afford a root canal yourself, but you might perform one this afternoon.

MINDSET IS THE FINAL TOOL

Lacey began to embrace this shift in view, particularly as we began to do so much better financially. She worked hard at it, going so far as to create "abundance alarms." She set her phone to go off at three-hour intervals with a message that said, "You are abundant. Money flows freely to you." That it was set as an alarm forced her to look at it when she shut it off.

Still, she was an anti-coin person. If she paid cash for something and received coins as change, she dismissed them as useless. She never bought anything with them, just set them aside somewhere, never to be used. She didn't respect the money in that form.

You must respect it in all forms. Just as it's important to have a great relationship with your clients and prospects, you must also have a great relationship with your money, where communication is the cornerstone of that relationship.

Can you imagine going on a ten-day trip and never once checking in with your significant other? It would not work wonders for your relationship. You're partners. You need to know how the other is doing in order to successfully maintain the relationship. The same holds true with your money.

I check in with my money every day as part of my morning routine, and not just as part of the administrative tasks of my day. Energetically, I check in to see how the accounts look each day.

Entrepreneurs, particularly those just starting out, tend to avoid this because perhaps the accounts are not looking so hot. Don't do that. Even when a relationship is in trouble with a partner, you don't check out. You open lines of communication because you need to be more in touch with them.

Treat your money well. If you like to accumulate actual cash, like I do, don't ball it up and stuff it in your pockets. Keep it in an organized wallet, bills facing the same way in order by denomination. Respect the money.

I know on the surface this sounds odd, but these are all exercises in changing your mindset such that you project yourself in a manner that allows money to flow freely to you from your clients. Lacey eventually began to take her accumulated coins to a Coinstar machine and convert them to cash. She stopped neglecting them. She recognized their value and the value of what respecting them meant.

When she did this, she too began to see money showing up all around her. Still, though her attitude toward coins improved, she didn't love them, and she struggled to pick them up.

At first.

She became so used to the practice, so committed to the idea, that one rainy day, as she exited her car, she saw a penny on the ground. As it was raining, the penny was wet, but when she went to pick it up, she discovered the coin was covered in spit. Instead of leaving it there, she tossed it back in the car, waited for it to dry, and added it to her jar to take to the Coinstar machine.

That's commitment. We attribute the majority of our success to the shift in mindset about money that we were both able to make.

Our relationship succeeds due in large part to our being

on the same page financially. If you have a significant other, it is vital that you are on the same page too. If you are living your life as an entrepreneur and your spouse views money as something that must be hoarded, if they're living a nine-to-five mindset, there is a potential for great turbulence in your relationship. You have to be eye-to-eye on how to grow the business.

That's a topic for another book.

DON'T CALL THE FINANCIAL PLANNER YET

Trust me when I tell you that you're going to be financially rewarded by this shift in mindset. One final strategy remains.

9

Support Is Conditional

The vision of this book is to help you as a service provider reach more people and be financially successful. So much so that you are able to give back.

Nothing makes us happier than when a client buys the home of their dreams and their dream car and takes that vacation they've always wanted, flying first class to get there. We want them to receive all of this so that they can give.

As your success grows, you can invest back into yourself, whether it is by self-development through continuing education or business development through expansion and scaling. What you'll realize is that your achievements may also be useful for other providers on their way up. You might now be in a position to serve as a mentor, and possibly even provide employment to a budding entrepreneur in a way that would be favorable financially, allowing them to cut into the learning curve, avoiding the mistakes you've made in your journey.

We believe in supporting all of the infrastructure that makes our professional lives possible. Those groups, those associations, those professional organizations need your support. There are colleges and trade schools. There are nonprofits that provide your service for underprivileged populations, both at home and abroad. You can support them with your time and talent.

It is, however, conditional.

YOU COULD IF YOU WOULD

If you find success and you hoard it, it will be short-lived. You have to learn to give, to support. Take a moment to take stock of and understand all of the things that got you where you are or where you're going. It is vital that you support them continuously on your journey. Put the give before the get. If you don't provide support until after you've applied everything you learned in this book, it's too late.

So many of you at this juncture might say, "That's great. I agree. I would if I could." That's not accurate.

You *could* if you *would*.

Think again about the people who sacrificed to get you where you are now, wherever that might be in your journey. There are a number of individuals who did, so many that you might not realize. Consider the instructors where you learned your trade, people who took the job because they had a passion for teaching, forgoing a possibly more lucrative career because they had a passion to help others learn.

If you practice in a profession that has licensing, have you stopped to think about what it took for that to occur? Did someone magically write the law requiring licensure, or did someone have to lobby for it? Was there a fight?

How were the schools and colleges you attended to learn your service formed? Did they spring up overnight or was sacrifice involved?

What about the pioneers in your field? Those who created the profession? Did someone laugh at the first dentist? The first physical therapist? What did it take for them to form an organization, to be taken seriously, in order for you to provide your service today?

We take these things for granted because they've been in place for so long. The people who paved the way for these opportunities have come and gone, but they all paid a price.

Never take that price for granted. You set the table to receive abundantly by supporting everywhere and every time that you're reasonably able. Everyone remembers when they first started out. A time when someone bought your lunch. Now you're in place to buy lunch for the person behind you.

If you attend seminars or continuing education events, look for the people new to the business. Reach out to them. Don't let your lack of financial abundance at the time be an excuse. Offer them advice and mentorship. That's free. The point is you have to start, and you have to do it now.

You can read this book, get something out of it, and watch your business explode. As we've said before, that's great. The only thing that could make us happier, how we know this book will truly have had an impact, would be to have you share that success.

What you'll find is that the more you give, the more you'll receive. It seems to be another one of those strange laws of the universe, but I've seen it happen time and time again. You receive through the same rip in the space-time continuum as you give, so give early, as soon as you're able. Everyone can give time. Everyone can share compassion. Everyone has the capacity to give in some form.

We are asking that if you find success or growth through the use of this book, don't jinx it. Multiply success by passing it down the line. Find further success by paying it forward to the rest of the world. We serve, and so the more you serve, the more you get paid. That's why we wrote this book specifically for you as the service professional. The more you serve, the more you gain.

IT'S NOT ONLY ABOUT THE MONEY

What you give comes back to you in ways that aren't strictly revenue based. You can receive service, favors, or doors opening for you where they'd been closed before. How do you put a monetary value on a timely introduction to a valued prospect or mentor? There are many ways to get paid.

We travel extensively, such that we're gone more than half the weekends in a year. Our seats are almost always upgraded, and it happens in proportion to the amount of giving we happen to be performing. Oftentimes, we will have a client for whom we have provided some financial assistance or that we've accommodated in some other way. This happened once for a client in Australia, where we travel twice a year. A first-class ticket to Australia costs upwards of $10,000, an amount in excess of what we would have earned from the client had we charged them full price. It happens that—way more often than not—where we don't just equal out, but the swing is in our favor.

This is not to say go out and give away your services. Of course, there may be times when you choose to do that, but make it an exception, not a rule. If you give something away, and you're doing it from the right place and mindset, you will see these opportunities line up. When they happen, don't dismiss it. Give credit to the universal balance from which it springs.

THE CHECK TEST

When someone offers to pick up the check at a meal, what do you do?

We are conditioned in our society to say no. We contend that when people offer to pick up the check, you must train yourself to say yes. Saying no is a pushback to the universe. Instead, just like with the coins on the street, show that you're open to more.

This isn't to say don't ever offer to pay. Sometimes you

can use it as a teachable moment, taking the opportunity to tell someone else that they should never refuse when someone offers to pay. Outside of that example, if you're offering to pay, it is because, in your subconscious mind, you are closed off to receiving. When people offer you things, accept them.

YOU DON'T OWE

It is a difficult programming to overcome because, in large part, we feel that in accepting something, we owe. In fact, there are a number of sales books and strategies that prey on this concept.

Consider this: in a lot of high-end sales, one of the key tactics is to offer your prospect something to drink, from a Coca-Cola to glass of champagne. Once, while in Australia, I went shopping for watches. The salesperson approached me to tell me about a special event they were holding that evening, during which they served beer and wine, and offered me a glass. I refused but continued to shop.

I knew which watch I wanted and eventually made the decision to buy it. I asked the seasoned veteran salesperson, "At what point do you know the sale has been made?" He responded that he thought we were doing well, that rapport had been established, but that at any moment I could get up and say I wanted to think about it and leave the store.

I told him in that moment that I wanted the watch and that I'd now take that glass of champagne. Had I taken it beforehand, I would have felt committed. I would have felt that I owed, no matter how disproportionate the value of the champagne to the value of the watch I was going to purchase.

Think back to the last time you bought a car. At some point during negotiations, did the dealer excuse himself to grab a coffee and offer to bring you one as well? If you accepted, you were closer to being closed than if you had said no. Had you refused, you would have been more comfortable walking out the door.

When you go to an open house, there are always cookies and other snacks. For the multimillion-dollar properties, they put out full-on spreads. They aren't doing this just to be accommodating. The deeper you go in, the more committed you are, the more you owe back. That's the mentality.

Train yourself out of that mentality. Be open to accepting. Don't fear it.

EXPECT A RETURN

Again, this concept is in direct opposition to how we've been conditioned to think. We are taught never to give with the expectation of something in return. I say it's just the opposite.

This doesn't mean that if I buy you lunch, I expect you to buy it the next time or to be reimbursed for the meal. However, I know I'll be repaid. I expect it, and when it shows up, I recognize it for what it is. I'll show up to the airport and be upgraded. A prospect will call and become a new client. All because I bought you lunch.

You can't only be a giver. You'll go broke and quickly. When you give, you must expect and be open to being replenished because energy flows into that void. As soon as you give, with the right intention and the right mindset, the universe will see to it that you are compensated.

We fully comprehend how difficult it is to overcome this programming, to not feel you owe. To give without expectation of getting. Start small. Help somebody on a lesser scale and watch it come back. Then test it repeatedly. You'll find that you cannot "out give" the phenomenon.

Always keep in mind that this is conditional. Don't give with frivolity. Direct your giving toward people and organizations that are in support of you, your family, and the way you make your living. Never do it out of a sense of obligation. Do it because you want to do it. That's how it comes back.

Now that we've addressed these crucial shifts in mindset, let's put a bow on it and send you off to serve your community.

Conclusion

STAY ON YOUR FEET

Let me take you back to Costa Rica for a moment.

With success come detractors. It's an unfortunate reality, but it's true. During my years running my practice, I found myself in need of a security detail to protect me when I moved from place to place. My life had been threatened on more than one occasion, to the point where I needed to take it quite seriously.

There is a significant amount of training you must undertake when working with a security team. You don't simply walk in a huddle of them. You must be prepared to take action and run if a situation gets dangerous. Without hyperbole, your life depends on the lessons these professionals teach you.

Without fail, the one that has stuck with me so many years later is this: stay on your feet. If the bullets start flying and you need to run, don't ever fall down. If you fall, you're dead.

As you reach the end of this book, this journey we took together, we encourage you to do the same. Stay on your feet. This doesn't mean don't fail—that your business will die if you experience failure. Instead, it is a reminder to never forget what you stand for. If you come back to this when you find yourself and your business in times of struggle, you will work your way out of that challenge.

It is our sincere hope that, at this stage, you are in touch with the enormity of your vision that you have for your service, who you are, what you have to offer the world, and the impact it has on people's lives.

In knowing that, we hope you now understand that you have to maintain a conviction stronger than your desire to please if you're going to be able to convert that vision into something more than just an idea or a dream—something that has the potential to change the world. Comprehend that in order to accomplish this, as you realize who you are and what you have to offer, you also have the ability to identify your ideal client, what it is they seek, and how you fit into that equation.

When you can do this, you become comfortable with

selling because you now know that selling is actually leading your prospect to the best decision they can make relative to their situation. Because you've made mindset changes relative to money, you're comfortable charging a fair amount for the service you provide in relation to the impact that it can make on your client's life. You do this not for your gain alone, and you remember that you can only achieve all of this if you give back to the very things that helped you get there.

THE SERVICE PROVIDER'S CREED

Create better success for yourself in order to provide your service to those who need it most.

Your community needs you as a service provider to be at your very best. That does not only mean financially but in your relationships, your mindset, emotionally, and spiritually. You do your best work not only when you're working with the ideal client but also when you're not worrying if the rent check will bounce. Being in a state of fear, worry, or anxiety relative to your business is not only unhealthy for you, but it's unfair to the clients you serve.

To be successful in business is not a self-centered ideal. We want you to be rich, of course. Who doesn't want that for themselves? We want it for you because we want you to be able to give back and because that financial security amplifies your ability to provide even greater service.

Imagine how incredible your service delivery would be if money were never an issue. You would only work with the people that you wanted to, and you would provide them with world-class service. You wouldn't look at your watch wondering how long you'd spent with them. You would provide your service until the end result was accomplished, whether it took five minutes or five hours.

That's the utopia of the service-provider world. Most people are searching for some degree of freedom. For some, it's financial freedom; for others, it's time. Creating financial abundance gives you both. When you achieve it, you must convert it. Take that extra time to increase your skillset by taking more courses. Spend more time with your clients. Invest in better equipment or facilities, better marketing or teams. Use that freedom to provide an even better service than you already do.

IMPLEMENTATION IS KEY

Jordan Belfort, the Wolf of Wall Street, once said, "'Should' is the most disempowering word in the English language."

If at any point in the reading of this book, you said to yourself, "I should do that," it's time for a reframe. If you took notes on any of the strategies laid out here, and if any of them say "should," go back and change them to "will." Tell yourself you will do these things.

If you don't, in a year from now, you'll be exactly where you are right now. It's that simple.

Take a moment and determine which of the strategies are ones that you're committed to implementing. It may not be all of them. It may only be one or two. Once you've implemented them and have integrated them into your service provision, tackle two more strategies on the list until you've used them all.

It is my hope that more advanced business readers will also find a handful of strategies to add to their arsenal. Utilize the Six Ps. Create goals. Set up rewards around accomplishing them. Share them and create accountability.

As service providers, we all know that there are elements of what we do that require our clients to engage independently to continue the benefits of our service. You can repair someone's refrigerator, but they're going to need to replace the water filter every six months. If they don't, the problem will arise again. If you're consulting your clients on nutrition and guide them to buy specific foods but they never buy them, they won't lose the weight.

You can read this book and come away with a number of great ideas, but if you don't do anything, then nothing changes.

Decide what you're going to do. Then do it.

JOIN OUR COMMUNITY

At the Black Diamond Club, we are not ashamed nor afraid of success. We are proud of the service that we provide to the world. We value our time and our expertise and have no problem being paid accordingly for the value we bring to the lives of those we touch. We believe that there is no one right way to do anything. We support each other and refuse to create hierarchies in the group. There is no one expert or authority on any subject.

In the end, we all have different definitions of success. There is room for us all to achieve our highest levels of potential, not only in our professions, but financially, with our families, and in the areas about which we are most passionate.

We practice discipline and focus. We don't waste time. We don't screw around. Frankly put, we get shit done, and we enjoy every minute of what we do. There is no other place we would rather be than where we are right now, and nothing else we would rather be doing than what we are doing right now.

We have uncompromising standards. We run our business and our lives knowing that "the standard is the standard."

We do realize support is conditional, and we appreciate yours in reading and (hopefully) sharing this book. To show you our appreciation, we invite you to join us. Lacey and I would like to buy you a three-month membership to the Black Diamond Club. To take us up on our offer, visit BlackDiamondClub.com/noyb.

Thank you for the service you provide to the world. We hope this book brings you the success you deserve.

Acknowledgments

It was Monday, July 31, 2017, when we met Jay Abraham in person for the very first time.

We were set to sit down with him to discuss our business and create a plan to take us to the next level. We had our metrics, our strategies, our relationships, our systems and processes—everything was ready to go.

We laid out everything we did and our vision for the future, and then the very thing Jay told us was that we needed a book.

"A book? No way! We're not writing a book!"

Thank you, Jay, for that little nudge. That nudge began this journey to create *None of Your Business*.

Looking back in order to see ahead, we are amazed at all of the steps that brought us to that creation point in Jay's office in Torrance, California.

We want to thank our parents, Hank and Marleen Dill and Laurie and Stanley "Bud" Book. They were always there and supported us when we were at our lowest points. It is easy to support now, but it takes the love of a parent to be there when things are rough and no one else is thinking about you.

We also want to mention our daughters, Mitsu and Miyoko Dill. They have become amazing businesswomen as they journey through their own paths of success. We have worked with them both in one way or another in our own business, and we have been taught many wonderful lessons as we observe the world through their "youthful" eyes!

Thanks to Eric Book and Chris Barrientos for being great brothers and allowing us to experience life through different lenses. Your stories and life adventures help us better understand the millennial perspective and outlook.

On the other side of July 31, many people have rallied their support to make this book happen.

Among those are Tristan Schaub, who believed that we

"had the belt" and knew to lie down so that the champs could elevate the promotion. In doing so, he introduced us to Tucker Max, who was invaluable in bringing this whole thing together. These two were the driving forces to taking an idea and bringing it to completion.

Then there are all of the doctors who work alongside us in the Specific Chiropractic Centers. They are the reason this book got done. They make everything possible in our lives. They carry the torch for our vision and are the "why" behind why we believe we were put on this earth.

Of course, we are eternally grateful for all of the members of the Black Diamond Club. It has been over five years together and we continue to grow. The Black Diamond Club has continued to serve as a giant lab where we are able to openly discuss these business concepts, test them in various markets and verticals, and strengthen our convictions.

In addition, we would like to thank our "illuminati" friends, Scott Garber, Jack Bourla, Steve Tullius, and Liam Schubel.

Hey, James and John...we did it! We never thought we would pull this off, but you two make dreams come true!

And in the end, we wish that our very good friend Andy

Roberts were still around to read this book. Andy was a constant in our lives until he was taken from us unexpectedly on June 11, 2016. We hope that this book is made available in heaven for you, our friend.

About the Author

DR. SHAWN DILL is a 1995 graduate of Logan College of Chiropractic. He is the CEO of the Specific Chiropractic Centers, which now operates fourteen Knee Chest Upper Cervical Specific clinics and also offers consulting services to entrepreneurs and healthcare professionals through his website, ShawnDill.com. Shawn is also the founder of the Black Diamond Club, a community committed to mentoring, motivation, and business development for service professionals.

Dr. Dill is a Certified Book Yourself Solid Coach under Michael Port, author of the best-selling book *Book Yourself Solid*. He offers his consulting services and workshops to empower service providers to embrace their inner entrepreneur and to achieve their business vision.

Shawn is a highly sought speaker, making numerous international appearances each year, and has been featured on radio and television programs around the world.

DR. LACEY BOOK has a passion to help service professionals reach more people through marketing, sales, and mindset strategies. She does this with her husband, Shawn, through the Black Diamond Club. She loves coaching service professionals who are just starting their businesses.

She is an international speaker and gives back by running three mission trips to other countries every year.

Learn more about Dr. Book at LaceyBook.com.

Made in the USA
Middletown, DE
17 September 2020

20079214R00097